TRANSIT AUTHORITY

THRU TRAINS RUN UP TO TŌBU DŌBUTSU KŌEN

TŌBU DŌBUTSU KŌEN

KITA-AYASE

ABIKO

MACHIYA — KITA-SENJU — AYASE

THRU TRAINS RUN UP TO ABIKO

AOTO

THRU TRAINS RUN ON KEISEI LINE

TABATA

NISHI-NIPPORI

MINAMI-SENJU

MINOWA

OSHIAGE

SENDAGI

NEZU

NIPPORI

UGUISUDANI

IRIYA

HONJOAZUMABASHI

YUSHIMA

INARICHŌ

UENO

ASAKUSA

UENOHIROKŌJI

OKACHIMACHI

TAWARAMACHI

SUEHIROCHŌ

NAKAOKACHIMACHI

KURAMAE

OGAWACHŌ

CHANOMIZU

AKIHABARA — ASAKUSABASHI

AWAJICHŌ

IWAMOTOCHŌ

MUSASHINO LINE

KANDA

OTEMACHI

SHIN-HOMBASHI

TSUDANUMA

BAKUROCHŌ

MITSUKOSHIMAE

BAKUROYOKOYAMA — HIGASHI-NIHOMBASHI — NISHI-FUNABASHI

TŌKYŌ

KODEMMACHŌ

THRU TRAINS RUN UP TO TSUDANUMA

NIHOMBASHI

BARAKINAKAYAMA

JŪBASHIMAE

NINGYŌCHŌ

GYŌTOKU

MINAMI-GYŌTOKU

UCHO

EDOBASHI

URAYASU

GINZAITCHŌME

KYŌBASHI

KASAI

GINZA

KAYABACHŌ

NISHI-KASAI

TAKARACHŌ

MINAMI-SUNAMACHI

SHINTOMICHŌ

HATCHŌBORI

KIBA

HIGASHI-GINZA

MONZENNAKACHŌ

TŌYŌCHŌ

TSUKISHIMA

TATSUMI

TSUKIJI

TOYOSU

SHIN-KIBA

▨ GINZA LINE	▨ YŪRAKUCHŌ LINE	⬤ Connecting to Subways
▨ MARUNOUCHI LINE	▨ HANZŌMON LINE	◯ Connecting to JNR and/or PRIVATE RAILWAYS
▨ HIBIYA LINE	▨ TOEI ASAKUSA LINE	▬ JNR
▨ TŌZAI LINE	▨ TOEI MITA LINE	— PRIVATE RAILWAYS
▨ CHIYODA LINE	▨ TOEI SHINJUKU LINE	

EATING CHEAP
IN JAPAN

**The Gaijin Gourmet's Guide to Ordering
in Non-tourist Restaurants**

by Kimiko Nagasawa
Camy Condon

SHUFUNOTOMO CO., LTD.
Tokyo, Japan

Cover Photo

The Beckoning Cat, "MANEKI-NEKO"

Decorative cats with one front paw raised to an ear are popular good luck charms which can be seen in many restaurants and shops. The origin is said to be a tale about Usugumo, a famous woman of Yoshiwara, whose favorite cat was killed as it tried to warn her of a dangerous snake. She had a copy of the cat carved from wood which became a famous charm and the first of the MANEKI-NEKO. Popular tradition says when a cat brushes its paw over its ear it is a sign that visitors will come. In his other paw he holds an ancient gold coin believed to bring riches to the MANNEKI-NEKO's owner.

First printing, 1972
20th printing, 1988

Published by Shufunotomo Co., Ltd.
2-9, Kanda Surugadai, Chiyoda-ku,
Tokyo, 101 Japan
Printed in Japan

ISBN4-07-971548-X

Acknowledgements

The authors wish to express their gratitude to the many people who assisted in the publication of this book. It is impossible to list everyone, but special mention must be given to the following people for their generous assistance: Holloway Brown, Atsushi Gohara, Kiyofumi Imai, Satoshi Ishii, Kikue Narita, Masako Sano, Tane Takahashi and Namiko Takeuchi. We are greatly indebted to the many restaurants all over Japan which provided the inspiration for this guide by their helpful service to foreign guests. In particular we would like to thank the following Tokyo restaurants for permission to photograph their foods: Azuma Zushi, Fukusuke, Restaurant Seibu, Sagano, Shisenhanten (Kanda), Shunko, Tokiwa, Yuzuki and Yabu. We are also grateful to two Tokyo department stores for information and assistance concerning the section on box lunches: Mitsukoshi (Ikebukuro branch) and Takashimaya. Finally, the authors wish to thank their hungry husbands who ate most of the foods recorded here and in many other ways made the completion of this book possible.

TABLE OF CONTENTS

INTRODUCTION

As a popular guide to Japan puts it, "Japan offers a greater variety of better, cleaner, more attractive, friendlier and above all cheaper restaurants than any other country in the world." The guide fails to say that few visitors to Japan and even many foreign residents ever take advantage of these inexpensive restaurants because so few can speak Japanese, let alone read a Japanese menu. And even those persons who claim to be able to "get by" in Japanese are likely to order the same three or four Japanese foods over and over because they are the only names they recognize or have tried.

This guide has been prepared to assist the person who doesn't know much (or any) Japanese but who enjoys good food, hopes to sample some of the extraordinary variety of Japanese dishes, wants to eat where the ordinary Japanese eats and not be surrounded by other foreigners, and who, incidentally, appreciates a bargain.

Our task is made easier because most of Japan's cheaper restaurants display extremely realistic wax models of the foods they serve in a window case outside near their entrances. (This commendable practice is said to have originated during the Meiji period when strange, new foods were being introduced along with everything else from the West. Today these wax models similarly serve the curious foreigner.) The wax models and the actual foods photographed for this guide will tell you what to anticipate when you order. However, you should be prepared for some modification in ingredients depending on the price of the dish, the size and location of the restaurant and the season.

It is our hope that this photographic and descriptive guide of the most frequently found and inexpensive Japanese foods will be your personal menu. Once you duck under the traditional restaurant doorway curtain, the NOREN, it can help you to sample some of the most representative dishes in this remarkable country.

This is *not* a guide to specific restaurants. Most of the dishes described in this guide can be found anywhere, probably within walking distance of wherever you are right now. If you lack imagination or don't know where you are, then look for the narrow streets surrounding any train station, check the shopping areas, wander in any neighborhood market section, look on one of the upper floors of any city department store or the lower floors (basements) of large office buildings. Japan abounds

3

with these delightful eateries. Very often housewives order foods from these restaurants delivered to their homes or apartments (which helps to explain how a three-table restaurant can continue to survive: they deliver). Often the little restaurants which serve many of the foods described here are single family establishments with the family living in the back two rooms. Almost all of the inexpensive restaurants you will want to try are simple, clean and very appealing—you can always peer inside first and avoid any spot that does not measure up to your standards.

This is also *not* a guide to exact prices. Since we hope this book will be helpful to you in all restaurants in all parts of Japan it is impossible to quote the prices of meals. The variations are too great and suggesting an average price for each dish would only invite confusion if it proved to be different from the one given next to the wax model or on your bill. Our favorite neighborhood Tempura restaurant, for example, offers a delicious TEMPURA TEISHOKU (see listing No. 16) of equal quality and better quantity than that served in one of Tokyo's finest hotels for exactly one-tenth of the price! Not all savings are this spectatular, nor do we mean to say that hotels overcharge the visitor. In fact, unlike some Western countries Japanese hotel food is excellent and highly recommended. But you do "get what you pay for," and if you want to pay for an English accent in your meals or for Western Foods you can eat at home, go right ahead. Another advantage is that small restaurants do not charge the special tax which is demanded in many establishments which serve tourists. And in no Japanese restaurants are you expected to leave a tip.

Most travelers agree that you cannot know a country without knowing the foods of the country. You may or may not "be what you eat," but at least what you eat is a part of your culture and reflects the geography, spirit and traditions of your country. We describe here the foods enjoyed or simply gulped down by businessmen, students, families and working people. Cheap restaurants are an integral part of daily life in the real Japan.

Are You Welcome?

The traditional sign of welcome to many inexpensive Japanese restaurants is the NOREN or slitted curtain which announces the kind of food served inside. As a rule, if the NOREN is hung out over the doorway the restaurant is open; if it is tucked inside, it is still closed. Almost everywhere you go to eat in Japan you

4

will be greeted with an "IRASHAIMASE" (Welcome!") as you enter. But if it is clear that the restaurant is open and you are not so warmly greeted, assume that the propieter is surprised by a non-Japanese face at the door and truly does not know what to say. You can credit this as a discovery—as can he— and hopefully with the help of this guide both of you will be pleased with the encounter. What the tourist often interprets as exclusiveness is more often caution in the face of uncertainty.

The Japanese are justly famous for avoiding embrassment and possible loss of face. We know of one excellent Osaka restaurant which closed during Expo '70 rather than risk a possible awkward encounter with foreign visitors. We also know of a restaurant, off the tourist track, which was surprised by foreign visitors but which was so delighted with their interest in Japanese foods that they entertained the visitors well into the night, exchanged names and addresses (though they shared no common language) and still keep in touch years later. Probably you will encounter neither extreme, but we hope you will use this guide and frequent many of the small restaurants which may have never before served a foreign guest.

On Being Filled Up

We have often heard it said that Japanese meals are not filling. It is also a common observation that, apart from Sumo wrestlers, one sees very few "fat Japanese." So let us offer a word on being "full." To begin with, Japanese food is prepared to be aesthetically pleasing. Great care is taken with the color and the arrangement of the foods and the matching of foods with tasteful and complementary dishes. In addition, Japanese meals offer a minimum of fatty foods like butter or olive oil, and fish (in relatively small quantities)—not meat—is the primary element of many meals. Yet another reason is the customary order of eating many meals, including the taking of rice as the final, and often main course, rather than as a starch complement to the rest of the foods.

Restaurants which cater to tourists often serve much less rice than do authentic Japanese restaurants, and even then the tourist is likely to leave some rice in the bowl saying he could not eat another bite, while across the street a Japanese customer has ordered a second or third helping. Then, too, there is what might be considered "the psychology of food," for in Japan a meal is not intended to simply fill one up and be nutritious; a proper meal whould be in every way appealing, a delight to the

5

eye and even to the ear. (What is the sound of one cracker crunching? one pickle snapping? one noodle slurping?)

Western Foods

We have not included the general category of "Western" (meaning European or American) foods which can be found in some types of inexpensive restaurants, with the exception of 3 or 4 extremely common foods like KARE RAISU (Curry Rice) which have become a part of standard Japanese food. Western meals, easily distinguished because the wax model meals are always shown on plates and platters instead of in bowls, seem to vary from place to place. We leave you on your own to guess at the ingredients by a careful examination of the models . . . . . (yes, that really *is* a serving of three spaghetti strands next to the hamburger patty!)

How to "Read" Japanese

The Japanese names of each dish in this guide are given in Romanized writing as well as in Japanese characters. It will be helpful in your ordering if you practice in advance the pronunciation of this writing system.

A . . . . 'ah' as in father, hot, box (not **a** as in at or ate).
E . . . . 'eh' as in enter, feather, met (not **e** as in beet).
I . . . . 'ee' as in eat, she, meat (not **i** as in it).
O . . . . 'oh' as in doe, go, so (not **o** as in pot).
U . . . . 'oo' as in pool, soup (not **u** as in up).
G . . . . hard 'G' as in get, girl, give (not **g** as in gem).
F . . . . you can read it as 'F' or 'H', the Japanese sound
is half-way between.

Japanese words are usually printed in capital letters whenever they occur throughout this guide. Consult the Glossary of Japanese Foods in the Appendix for definitions of unfamiliar ingredients. In the food listings the name of each dish is written twice, the second time with dashes to assist your pronunciation of each syllable.

A caution about words which begin with O. In polite conversation some words are given an honorific 'O' which sounds like it is the first letter of the word. For example, O-SOBA (buckwheat noodles), O-HASHI (chopsticks), O-SAKE (Japanese rice wine), O-MOCHI (rice cakes). If you can't locate the food in our listing under the 'O' sound, then look up the name beginning with the second letter.

TYPES OF JAPANESE RESTAURANTS

1. SOBA-YA*—The Japanese Noodle Shop

(SO–BA–YA)

*The "YA" means shop, place or house

This is the place for many kinds of Japanese noodle dishes which are especially popular at lunch time. Most of the wax models in the display case show bowls of noodles in a standard soup with various combinations of vegetables and meat or fish on the top. In addition to a variety of these hot and cold noodle dishes, you can also order a few of the most popular Chinese noodle dishes and simple rice meals. Sometimes two or three of the very popular Western style foods are also on the menu.

A Hint: You can usually tell a noodle by its container . . . and other foods too.

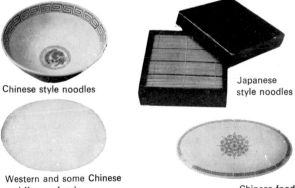

Chinese style noodles

Japanese style noodles

Western and some Chinese and Korean foods

Chinese food

7

2. KORYŌRI-YA—The Restaurant for Traditional Japanese Foods

(KO–RYŌ–RI–YA)

These are exclusively Japanese restaurants which offer a variety of seasonal, fresh fish and vegetable dishes served in the traditional style. Most of the dishes found in these restaurants are listed under our section "A La Carte Dishes and Snacks." These restaurants are also popular places to drink SAKE and beer, while sampling the many kinds of appetizers especially prepared to be eaten with drinks. This type of restaurant is often small, but it is likely to have a few semi-private, tatami-mat rooms for small parties. Sometimes these restaurants have a folk-craft decor, and they may or may not have a wax model display of their foods.

Fish and vegetable dishes served in traditional Japanese style are the offerings in a KORYŌRI-YA.

3. SHOKUJI DOKORO*—The Very Small Restaurant for Traditional Japanese foods

(SHO–KU–JI DO–KO–RO)

* Sometimes called MESHI-YA (ME–SHI–YA)

This is a smaller version of the KORYŌRI-YA usually displaying wax models to advertise a limited menu. These restaurants are frequently very, very small shops with a counter and perhaps three or four tables or tatami-mat booths. The menu offerings are usually limited to a few of the traditional and most popular Japanese dishes.

8

The SHOKUJI DOKO-RO: a limited menu of the most popular Japanese foods.

4. **SUSHI-YA**—The SUSHI Shop Specializing in Seasoned Rice and Fresh, Raw Fish, etc. See page 38.

(SU–SHI–YA)

The SUSHI Shop may be the most distinctive of all small Japanese restaurants. Seasoned rice in rolls, slices, mounds and bowls topped with slices of raw, or occasionally cooked, fish and sometimes vegetables is the specialty. You may order individual pieces (see NIGIRI ZUSHI, Nos. 68–88) or plate combinations.

The SUSHI Shop

A counter seat permits individual selection of SUSHI.

5. CHŪKA RYŌRI-YA—The Inexpensive Chinese Restaurant

(CHŪ–KA–RYŌ–RI–YA)

This is the category of inexpensive, Chinese style restaurants which offer very popular Japanese versions of Chinese dishes. There are many expensive and authentic Chinese restaurants in Japan, but our listing is limited to the more modest and popular variety which is always found in the same shopping and neighborhood locations as the SOBA-YA and SUSHI-YA.

6. SHOKUDŌ—The "Mixed" Restaurant

(SHO–KU–DŌ)

This is the small, inexpensive, general restaurant which offers a mixed group of foods: (a) a few of the most popular Chinese noodle dishes, (b) a few Western rice dishes, (c) a limited selection of Japanese rice dishes and (d) a few desserts. There is always a case displaying the menu offerings. This is one of the favorite eateries of college students living away from home and single businessmen.

7. SPECIALTY RESTAURANTS

In the larger Japanese cities there are many kinds of restaurants and small eateries which serve, or at least specialize in, one particular food. Some of these places are very small and very cheap, while others can be expensive depending on the specialty, the location and the clientele. Most of these restaurants are very common; the few less frequently found places are marked "*."

a. Very Small and Very Cheap:

(Each of these eateries is the same name as its particular food specialty. See the food listing for a description. The number refers to each food.

```
OCHAZUKE-YA  ....  10
ODEN-YA  .......... 123
OKONOMI-YAKI-YA 151
ONIGIRI-YA  ........  12
YAKITORI-YA  ...... 140
ZŌSUI  .............  24
```

b. Larger, Moderately Priced:

```
KAMAMESHI-YA....   5
*KUJIRA-YA  ........    Whale meat specialty
TEMPURA-YA  ......  15 & 16
TONKATSU-YA  ....136 Pork cutlet specialty
TORI-YA  ............    Chicken specialty
UNAGI-YA .......... 19—22  Eel specialty
```

c. Likely to be Expensive:

```
BEEF (GYŪ NIKU)    Beef specialty
SUKIYAKI-YA  ......153⎫ Dishes cooked
TEPPAN YAKI  ......154⎭   at your table
*FUGU  .............    Blowfish specialty
KANI  .............    Crab specialty
*SUPPON  ...........    Snapping turtle specialty
KYŌDO RYŌRI  ....    Restaurants which offer regional,
                     "country style" home cooking.
                     Fresh fish and vegetables are
                     brought daily from the country-
                     side to prepare the particular
                     house specialty.
```

8. NOMI-YA—Neighborhood Bar Which Offers Some Light Meals and Snacks

(NO–MI–YA)

This is a very broad category including a variety of local bars, very often incredibly small (perhaps a single counter with only 5 stools). The emphasis is on drinking beer and SAKE, but a variety of snacks and special appetizers are always available.

A NOMI-YA can often be recognized by a large, red, paper lantern hanging near the door.

Inside one drinks SAKE or beer and nibbles a variety of fish, vegetable and cracker snacks.

KANMI–YA
Japanese style desserts

KŌHĪTEN
A coffee shop

9. KISSATEN—The Place for Desserts, Snacks, Soft Drinks, Coffee and Tea

(KIS-SA-TEN)

Several types of restaurants are grouped together under this heading:

KŌHĪ SHOPPU KŌHĪ TEN	"Coffee Shop," usually small, emphasis on coffee, tea and soft drinks.
TEA ROOM	Western style desserts & drinks.
KANMI-YA SHIRUKO-YA	Japanese style desserts, snacks and drinks.

There are a great variety of these modern and traditional tea rooms and coffee shops. Some specialize in coffee and classical music or jazz (popular with young people and students who sit for hours over coffee while studying), others offer a great variety of ice cream desserts, and still others provide an elaborate menu which includes light meals as well as desserts. Some are places for purely traditional Japanese snacks with an amazing assortment of bean desserts. Others offer both Western and Japanese style foods.

13

OTHER KINDS OF
RESTAURANTS

To complete our description of restaurant types, we must mention several kinds of restaurants which serve dishes *NOT* included in our photographic listings, either because they are expensive or Western.

Perhaps the loveliest and most interesting of the expensive restaurants are the **RYŌTEI**, offering elaborate full course Tokyo and Kyoto style foods usually accompanied by traditional Japanese entertainment; and restaurants serving **KAI-SEKI RYŌRI**, featuring delicate and beautiful foods served during the formal Tea Ceremony meal. You are not likely to recognize either of these as restaurants because they look like lovely private homes or traditional Japanese inns with only a very modest sign to identify them as restaurants. It is almost always necessary to have reservations in advance at these places, and sometimes you will need a personal introduction to the establishment even before the reservation is possible.

Two modifications of the cooking style found in the above restaurants are: **KYŌ RYŌRI**, which are the particularly elaborate dishes popular in the Kyoto-Osaka district, and **SHŌJIN RYŌRI**, vegetarian foods artfully arranged and served in some Buddhist temples.

Another usually expensive restaurant type is the **KAPPŌ**. Here, fresh seasonal fish and vegetables combining Tokyo and Kyoto cooking styles are the specialty. There is often little or no selection of dishes involved; rather, the establishment selects and serves the full course meal of the day. Some Japanese Inns advertise themselves as **KAPPŌ RYOKAN**, meaning they pride themselves on their special meals.

Finally, a word about Western foods. The **RESUTORAN** and **YŌSHOKU-YA** are usually inexpensive restaurants which are as close as you will come to cheap "home cooking" Western style. These places specialize in Japanese imitations of European and American style cooking. You can easily distinguish this kind of restaurant because of the use of plates and platters instead of bowls in the wax model display. As these dishes are not standardized, and frequently not so very cheap, we have not included them in our listing. (Also, you can always eat this kind of food at home.) Some of these Western plate combinations may come as a surprise to the newly arrived foreigner, such as tiny servings of potatoes and vegetables, or the usual choice of bread *or* rice, while others may amuse the visitor, like potato salad-filled hot dog buns, and cold pork cutlet hamburgers.

SUNAKKU (SU-NAK-KU), from the English "Snack."

a. The Daytime SUNAKKU is a very small version of the RESUTORAN with a menu limited to a few light meals like spaghetti, sandwiches, a hamburger patty plate and a few desserts. Soft drinks and beer are also available. During the day this kind of restaurant is popular with shoppers and mothers with young children.

b. Night-time SUNAKKU. The evening version of this same kind of restaurant developed as a means of getting around the mandatory closing hours for bars and clubs. Since there is no limit to how late a restaurant may stay open, the night-time SUNAKKU is legally a "restaurant" although it is socially a bar. Beer, mixed drinks and SAKE are served along with a limited number of Western style light meals.

SHOJIN RYORI:
vegetarian dishes
served on formal
lacquer trays.

RICE DISHES

1. CHĀ HAN　チャーハン　　　　　　　Hot

▷ Shokudō　Chinese Restaurant

Fried rice mixed with small pieces of pork (sometimes shrimp or crab too), onions, cooked egg, fish cake and peas. It is often served with a small bowl of clear soup.

2. CHŪKA DONBURI　中華どん　　　　　Hot

▷ Shokudō　Chinese Restaurant

A plate or bowl of rice covered with a thick, clear sauce usually containing a few pork pieces, bamboo shoots, a quail egg, carrot and onion slices and Chinese cabbage or pea pods. Sometimes slices of boiled squid are included. This dish is also called CHŪKAHAN.

3. HANGETSU......See No. 8 MAKU NO UCHI

4. HAYASHI RAISU　ハヤシライス　　　　Hot

▷ Shokudō　Yōshoku-ya

Small pieces of sliced beef and onions in a gravy poured over a mound of rice. (It is eaten with a spoon.)

5. KAMAMESHI　かまめし　　　　　　　Hot

▷ Shokuji Dokoro　Kamameshi-ya　Kanmi-ya

Rice steamed in fish bouillon seasoned with soy sauce. Small pieces of chicken (TORI), crab (KANI) or shrimp (EBI) are mixed with bits of bamboo shoot, mushrooms, and peas. This special rice is steamed and served in a delightful clay pot with a wooden lid set into a wooden serving box.

6. KARĒ RAISU　カレーライス　　　　　Hot

▷ Shokudō　Soba-ya, Udon-ya　Yōshoku-ya

Rice with a curry-flavored "stew" poured over the top. The stew usually contains a few pieces of pork (sometimes other meat), potatoes and onions with a few red pickles (imitation chutney) or pickled ginger slices on the side. (This is one of the most popular and cheapest of the foreign foods which has become a standard "Japanese" dish.) No condiments are sprinkled over the top.

7. KATSU DON　カツどん　　　　　　　Hot

▷ Shokudō　Soba-ya, Udon-ya

A bowl of rice topped with one deep-fried, breaded and sliced pork cutlet cooked in egg with a few peas and onions. A small dish of pickles is usually served on the side.

16

1. CHĀ-HAN

2. CHŪ-KA DON-BU-RI

4. HA-YA-SHI RA-I-SU

5. KA-MA-ME-SHI

6. KA-RĒ RA-I-SU

7. KA-TSU DON

8. MAKU NO UCHI 幕の内 Cold
▷ Kappō Shokuji Dokoro Box Lunch—EKI BEN

This is a kind of traditional Japanese picnic lunch. Small rice rolls sprinkled with black sesame seeds are in one section. Other sections contain a piece of broiled fish or shrimp, an egg slice, a few vegetables and pickles. It is sometimes served in a half-circle shaped lacquered box and because of this it is also called HAN-GETSU ("Half Moon") This lunch originated as a meal to be eaten between the acts of the long Kabuki plays.

9. NIKU DON 肉どん Hot
▷ Shokudō Soba-ya, Udon-ya

A bowl of rice with a few slices of beef, onions, TOFU and gelatin noodles cooked in a sweetened soy sauce which is poured over the top. It is a kind of individual, ready-made SUKIYAKI. It is often served with a side dish of pickles.

10. OCHAZUKE· お茶漬け Hot
▷ Shokuji Dokoro Nomi-ya Sunakku Ochazuke-ya

A bowl of rice over which has been poured a fish or tea broth. NORI squares and trefoil leaves are sometimes on top. There are four varieties depending on an additional ingredient:

1. Salted Salmon: SAKE CHAZUKE
2. White Fish: TAI or FUGU CHAZUKE
3. Pickles: TSUKEMONO CHAZUKE
4. Dried Seaweed: NORI CHAZUKE
5. Raw Tuna: MAGURO CHAZUKE (or SASHIMI CHAZUKE)

A dab of green horseradish will be on the underside of the bowl's lid; mix this into the rice if you like. This dish is a light snack, often eaten after drinking or sometimes as the last dish of a dinner.

11. OMURAISU オムライス Hot
▷ Shokudō Soba-ya, Udon-ya

A plain omelet wrapped around rice which has been mixed with tomato sauce, and a few pork or chicken pieces. Ketchup usually decorates the top.

12. ONIGIRI おにぎり Cold
▷ Nomi-ya Onigiri-ya

Usually three rice triangles (or balls) wrapped with a strip of dried seaweed, and containing either a pickled plum, UME-BOSHI, a small piece of salted salmon, SAKE, or a bit of cooked pink codfish eggs, TARAKO, in the center. This is the most common Japanese picnic food and snack and is a favorite of children.

8. MA-KU NO U-CHI

9. NI-KU DON

10. O-CHA-ZU-KE

11. O-MU-RA-I-SU

12. O-NI-GI-RI

13. OYAKO DONBURI 親子どんぶり Hot
▷ Shokudō Soba-ya, Udon-ya

A bowl of rice covered with pieces of chicken and onion cooked in egg. Some dried seaweed decorates the top. A small dish of pickles is sometimes served on the side. (The Japanese name means "parent and child.")

14. TAMAGO DONBURI 卵どんぶり Hot
▷ Shokudō Soba-ya, Udon-ya

A bowl of rice topped with sliced onions cooked in egg and decorated with dried seaweed. It is one of the cheapest rice dishes.

15. TEMPURA 天ぷら

16. TEMPURA TEI SHOKU 天ぷら定食 Hot
▷ Tempura-ya Shokuji Dokoro Koryōri-ya

A variety of beautifully arranged and delicately prepared deep-fried foods. Usually some of the following are included: one or two shrimp or prawns, a piece of squid and white fish, eggplant, green pepper, onion, sweet potato, string beans, a NORI square and an edible leaf (beefsteak plant). A thin dip is served on the side. Mix the bit of grated radish into the dip and eat each piece of TEMPURA after dipping it into this. TEISHOKU means a meal of prearranged course. The plate of TEMPURA is served with a bowl of rice, soup and pickles.

17. TEN DON 天どん Hot
▷ Shokudō Soba-ya, Udon-ya

A bowl of rice with one or two deep-fried shrimp TEMPURA on top. The shrimp have been dipped in a soy sauce broth and are not as crispy as regular TEMPURA. Some of the broth is poured over the rice. A small dish of pickles is served on the side.

18. TONKATSU RAISU......See No. 136 TONKATSU

19. UNAGI DONBURI うなぎどんぶり Hot
Broiled eel served over rice in a bowl.

20. UNAGI KABAYAKI うなぎかば焼き Hot
Charcoal broiled eel.

21. UNAJŪ うな重 Hot
Broiled eel served over rice in a lacquered box.

13. O-YA-KO DON-BU-RI

14. TA-MA-GO DON-BU-RI

16. TEM-PU-RA TEI-SHO-KU

17. TE-N DO-N

19. U-NA-GI DON-BU-RI

21. U-NA-JŪ

21

22. UNAGI TEISHOKU うなぎ定食 Hot

A full course broiled eel meal which includes clear soup and pickles.

▷ Unagi-ya Shokuji Dokoro

Charcoal broiled eel is a delicacy equally appreciated by the foreign guest and Japanese host. This delicious food is best sampled at a restaurant which specializes in eel (UNAGI-YA) as good cooking requires skill and experience. (These restaurants are very common, particularly in Tokyo.) The best eels are grown naturally in rivers and ponds, although today many are raised artificially because of their great popularity.

Eels should be kept alive until cooking. Then the bone is removed and the eel pieces are arranged on bamboo skewers over a charcoal fire. After broiling they are usually steamed to soften the meat and then broiled again. During this second broiling process the meat is dipped several times into a special, sweet sauce. The prices of eel vary depending upon the size and how it is raised. The best eel is so good it is wise to order the most expensive cut, ICHIBAN JŌTŌ. A special seasoning made of powdered pepper leaves called SANSHO is considered essential by Tokyo eel lovers. It is available in a small shaker on the table.

23. WA TEISHOKU 和定食 Hot & Cold

▷ Koryōri-ya Shokuji Dokoro

A very general name meaning Japanese-style meal. What is included depends on the restaurant. TEISHOKU means full course which includes rice, soup, a little fish and vegetable dish, pickles and tea. Sometimes there may be a choice of WA-TEISHOKU MATSU or WA-TEISHOKU TAKE. (See MATSU, TAKE, UME explanation on page 42.)

24. ZŌSUI ぞうすい Hot

▷ Koryōri-ya Sunakku

Rice boiled in a soup seasoned with soy sauce. Trefoil, egg, oysters (KAKI) or crab (KANI) are sometimes mixed in. This kind of rice soup is often cooked in the stock of a one-pot meal and is made and eaten at the end of the dinner.

22. U-NA-GI TEI-SHO-KU   24. ZŌ-SU-I

NOODLE DISHES

"What's in a Noodle . . . . . ?"

Inexpensive restaurants in Japan are a great find for the budget-minded noodle lover. The variety of Japanese noodle dishes (found in the SOBA-YA or UDON-YA) and Chinese noodle dishes (in the CHŪKA RYŌRI-YA or SHOKUDŌ) will delight the most discriminating connoisseur, and the price will amaze you. A large luncheon bowl can be had for 40 or 50 cents (U.S.) Proper Japanese noodle eating etiquette requires making a noisy slurping sound as you eat. It is a good idea to have some tissues or a clean handkerchief with you when you eat noodles as napkins or little damp towels (OSHIBORI) are not a part of the noodle restaurant's hospitality.

Most hot Japanese style noodle dishes are accompanied by a small dish of leek slices to be added as a spice. A container of very spicy mixed red pepper and seasonings is also on the table for your use. The hot soup which remains after the noodles are eaten may be drunk directly from the bowl. (A Chinese spoon is provided for the soup in Chinese noodle dishes, but no spoon is given with Japanese noodles.)

Noodles are conveniently divided into two categories: Japanese noodles which are brownish or white noodles in various widths and thicknesses, and Chinese noodles, standard yellowish noodles eaten boiled or fried.

I. JAPANESE NOODLES

    a.   SOBA . . . . .Long, brownish-gray noodles made
            O-SOBA (polite)   from buckwheat flour. They have a
            NIHON SOBA   square   shape   and   originated   in

Japan. Before the Edo period a buckwheat dumpling was used as a substitute for rice by mountain people. Buckwheat could be cultivated in the less fertile mountain soil and could be harvested twice a year. At the beginning of the Edo period a way was discovered to convert the dumpling mixture into a noodle. Eggs and potato starch or a special root were mixed with the flour to produce a dough suitable for cutting into strips. Today many places pride themselves on serving regional, home-made O-SOBA. There are three major varieties of O-SOBA restaurants, SARASHINA, YABU and SUNA-BA, each specializing in a slight variation of the SOBA making process. SOBA is often eaten cold in a noodle shop which makes and cuts the noodles by hand. (Some very popular yellow Chinese noodle dishes are mistakenly called SOBA).

b. UDON .... Long, white, wide noodles made from
O-UDON (polite) wheat flour. Some noodle dishes can be made with either SOBA or UDON, the customer should specify.

c. HIYA MUGI .... Thin, white, long noodles made from wheat flour and served chilled in the summer season.

d. SŌMEN .... A very, very thin, long, white noodle made from wheat flour. It is usually served floating in a bowl of cold water during the summer season.

e. HIMO KAWA .. Wide, long, thin, white noodles made from wheat flour. Called KISHI-MEN in the Kyoto-Osaka area.

II. CHINESE NOODLES

Chinese noodles can be found in several cooking styles, boiled or fried but there is really only one kind of noodle. It is long, thin and light yellow in color and is made from flour, egg, salt and a special mineral water called KANSUI.

25. ANKAKE UDON
あんかけうどん　　　Hot

▷ Soba-ya, Udon-ya

Noodles (specify UDON or SOBA) served in a bowl covered with a thick sauce made from fish bouillon seasoned with soy sauce. Two or three fish cake slices, a mushroom, a slice of bamboo shoot, a piece of FU and a bit of spinach are usually in the sauce. (Winter season only.)

25. AN-KA-KE U-DON

26. CHAN PON　チャンポン　　　　　Hot

▷ Chinese Restauraut　Shokudō

Chinese noodles in a salted bouillon soup. A few pieces of pork, Chinese cabbage, bamboo shoots, bean sprouts and KIKU-RAGE are cooked in a thick sauce and then poured over the top. Sometimes bits of cooked egg are included in the soup.

27. CHĀSHŪ MEN　チャーシューメン　　　Hot

▷ Shokudō　Chinese Restaurant

Chinese noodles in pork bouillon seasoned with soy sauce. Four or five slices of pork are arranged (usually in a circle) on top of the noodles. A little spinach or a few peas are often added for color. Sometimes leek slices and Chinese bamboo are included.

26. CHAN PON　　　　　27. CHĀ-SHŪ-MEN

28. CHA SOBA 茶そば
> Soba-ya, Udon-ya

Tea-flavored green noodles (buckwheat) served on a bamboo rack in a lacquered box. A soy sauce broth comes in a small bottle on the side, and another tiny dish contains a few leek slices and a dab of horseradish. Mix the condiments into the broth using the box or bowl provided and then dip the noodles in a few at a time before slurping politely. After you have eaten the noodles you may request "SOBA-YU," the hot water in which the noodles have been boiled. A little of this will be poured into your remaining broth dip dish. This then becomes a final soup.

29. CHIKARA UDON 力うどん   Hot

> Soba-ya, Udon-ya

UDON noodles in a fish broth seasoned with soy sauce. Two pieces of rice cake (MOCHI), pressed fish cake slices or bits of fried flour crusts are on top. A little spinach or leek may be added for color.

30. GOMOKU SOBA 五目そば

> Shokudō Soba-ya, Udon-ya Chinese Restaurant

Chinese noodles in a pork broth. On top are various foods: usually half a hard boiled egg or a whole quail egg, a few pork or Chinese ham slices, 2 or 3 fish cake slices, sometimes shrimp, a few pea pods or a bit of spinach, bamboo shoot slices and a few pieces of Chinese cabbage or carrot. A few very small pieces of pork or ham are mixed into the soup. This is one of the most popular Japanese-style Chinese dishes.

31. GYŌZA SOBA ギョーザそば   Hot

> Shokudō Chinese Restaurant

Chinese noodles in a soy sauce seasoned pork broth. Three or four GYŌZA (see listing No. 163) are on the top. Sometimes a bit of spinach and a few leeks are also included.

32. HIMOKAWA ひもかわ   Hot

> Soba-ya, Udon-ya

KISHIMEN noodles in a fish broth seasoned with soy sauce. A bit of spinach and some dried, shaved bonito, fish cake slices and fried thin TŌFU strips are on the top. This dish is popular in Nagoya.

28. CHA SO-BA

29. CHI-KA-RA U-DON

30. GO-MO-KU SO-BA

31. GYŌ-ZA SO-BA

32. HI-MO-KA-WA

27

Noodle Dishes

33. HIYAMUGI　冷やむぎ　Cold

▷ Soba-ya, Udon-ya　Shokudō

Long, thin, white noodles served in a bowl of cold water with
a few ice cubes, a cherry and a bit of cucumber floating on the
top. (You're not expected to drink the water.) Pick up a few
strands with your chopsticks and dip them into the small dish
of soy sauce broth on the side before eating. (Summer season
only.)

34. HIYASHI CHŪKA　冷やし中華　Cold

▷ Soba-ya, Udon-ya　Shokudō　Chinese Restaurant

Chinese noodles served on a plate with a cold sauce made from
sesame seed oil, vinegar, sugar, soy sauce and red pepper. Thin
strips of cucumber, ham, fish cake and red, pickled ginger are
in sections on the top. This dish is also called HIYASHI SOBA
or HIYASHI RĀMEN. (Summer season only.)

35. ITAME SOBA......See No. 64 YAKI SOBA

36. KAKE SOBA　かけそば　Hot

▷ Soba-ya, Udon-ya

Noodles (specify SOBA or UDON) in a fish broth seasoned with
soy sauce. This is the cheapest kind of SOBA. Leek slices and
pepper can be used as a seasoning.

37. KAMO NANBAN　かも南蛮　Hot

▷ Soba-ya, Udon-ya

Noodles (specify SOBA or UDON) in a fish bouillon seasoned
with soy sauce. Several small pieces of chicken and slices of leek
are served on the top.

38. KANTON MEN　広東めん　Hot

▷ Chinese Restaurant　Shokudō

Chinese noodles in a salted, pork flavored soup. Small pieces of
pork, cabbage, carrots, bamboo shoots, mushrooms and sometimes a quail egg are in a thick sauce poured over the top.

39. KARĒ NANBAN　カレー南蛮　Hot

▷ Soba-ya, Udon-ya

UDON noodles in a curry flavored soup with a few pieces of
pork or beef mixed in.

40. KISHI MEN......See No. 32 HIMOKAWA

28

33. HI-YA-MU-GI

34. HI-YA-SHI CHŪ-KA

36. KA-KE SO-BA

37. KA-MO NAN-BAN

38. KAN-TON MEN

39. KA-RĒ NAN-BAN

29

41. KISHI ZARU　きしざる　　　　　Cold
▷ Soba-ya, Udon-ya

KISHIMEN noodles with dried seaweed strips on the top. A soy sauce seasoned soup dip is served in a bottle together with a small dish of condiments. Mix the soup and spices into the small bowl provided and dip the noodles into this a few at a time.

42. KITSUNE UDON　きつねうどん　　　　Hot
▷ Soba-ya, Udon-ya

Noodles (specify SOBA or UDON) in a fish broth seasoned with soy sauce. A few pieces of fried TOFU and leeks are arranged on the top. (In Japanese legends fried TOFU is known to be the favorite food of the KITSUNE, a sly fox, which is said to live in a forest called Shinoda.)

43. MISO NIKOMI UDON　みそ煮込みうどん　　Hot
▷ Soba-ya, Udon-ya　Koryōri-ya

UDON noodles boiled in a fish broth seasoned with MISO. A few pork (sometimes beef) slices are usually included along with leeks and a single large mushroom. Sometimes gelatin noodles and FU are also added. This dish is prepared and served in a small earthenware pot. (Winter season only.)

44. MISO RĀMEN　みそラーメン　　　　Hot
▷ Shokudō　Chinese Restaurant

Chinese noodles in a pork broth seasoned with soy sauce and MISO. A few pork pieces and bean sprouts are on top, and sometimes a little spinach and Chinese bamboo pieces are added.

45. MORI SOBA　もりそば　　　　　Cold
▷ Soba-ya, Udon-ya

Japanese buckwheat noodles served cold on a bamboo rack in a lacquered box. A sweetened soy sauce dip is served in a small bowl along with a tiny dish of condiments. Put these spices into the broth and dip a few strands of the noodles into the mixture before slurping appreciatively in the polite manner.

46. MOYASHI SOBA　もやしそば　　　　Hot
▷ Shokudō　Chinese Restaurant　Rāmen Stand

Chinese noodles, mistakenly called SOBA, in a pork broth flavored with soy sauce. Bean sprouts (MOYASHI) and sometimes a few other vegetables are sautéed and then arranged over the top of the noodles.

41. KI-SHI ZA-RU

42. KI-TSU-NE U-DON

43. MI-SO NI-KO-MI U-DON

44. MI-SO RĀ-MEN

45. MO-RI SO-BA

46. MO-YA-SHI SO-BA

47. NABE YAKI UDON　なべ焼きうどん　　　　Hot
▷ Soba-ya, Udon-ya

UDON noodles in a fish broth seasoned with soy sauce. One large mushroom, slices of bamboo shoot, FU, a little bunch of spinach and a fish cake or two are arranged on the top. Sometimes one shrimp TEMPURA and half a hard boiled egg are also included. This food is served in an individual casserole dish with a lid. (Winter season only.)

48. NAMEKO UDON　なめこうどん　　　　Hot
▷ Soba-ya, Udon-ya

Noodles (specify SOBA or UDON) in a fish bouillon seasoned with soy sauce. Many small, round mushrooms (NAMEKO) and a bit of spinach or trefoil leaves, dried seaweed and grated radish are served on the top.

49. NIKOMI UDON......See No. 47 NABE YAKI UDON

50. NIKU NANBAN　肉南蛮　　　　Hot
▷ Soba-ya, Udon-ya

Noodles (specify SOBA or UDON) in a fish bouillon seasoned with soy sauce. Several thin slices of pork (occasionally beef) and leeks are placed on the top.

51. OKAME SOBA　おかめそば　　　　Hot
▷ Soba-ya, Udon-ya

Noodles (SOBA or UDON) in a fish bouillon seasoned with soy sauce. Two or three fish cake slices, a mushroom, a slice of bamboo shoot, one or two wheat cakes (FU) and a bit of spinach or trefoil leaves are usually arranged over the noodles.

52. RĀMEN　ラーメン　　　　Hot
▷ Chinese Restaurant　Shokudō, Soba-ya, Udon-ya
Street and Festival Food

Chinese noodles in pork broth seasoned with soy sauce. One or two bits of thinly sliced pork and ham strips, a bit of spinach and sliced leeks are usually on top. The cheapest variety may have a few pieces of Chinese bamboo instead of the meat. RĀMEN is the most popular and cheapest Japanese style Chinese food. "Instant" packaged RĀMEN is a favorite for light meals at home.

53. SHINODA......See No. 42 KITSUNE UDON

47. NA-BE YA-KI U-DON

48. NA-ME-KO U-DON

50. NI-KU NAN-BAN

51. O-KA-ME SO-BA

52. RĀ-MEN

33

54. SŌMEN　そうめん　　　　　　　　　　　　　Cold
▷　Shokuji Dokoro　Soba-ya, Udon-ya　Koryōri-ya

Very, very thin white noodles usually served floating in cold
water in a large glass bowl. Ice cubes, a single cherry, a few
slices of cucumber, a piece of tomato and sometimes a shrimp
all add to the effect of a cooling summer meal. The noodles are
to be lifted out of the water a few at a time and dipped into your
individual bowl of soy sauce seasoned broth. This dish looks
like HIYAMUGI; see listing No. 33. (Summer season only.)

55. TAMAGO TOJI　卵とじ　　　　　　　　　　　　Hot
▷　Soba-ya, Udon-ya

UDON noodles served in fish bouillon seasoned with soy sauce.
Cooked egg and a piece of dried seaweed and fish cake are
arranged on the top. Sliced leeks and grated horseradish may
be used as seasonings.

56. TANMEN　たんめん　　　　　　　　　　　　　Hot
▷　Shokudō　Chinese Restaurant

Chinese noodles in a pork broth with a few vegetables, usually
Chinese cabbage, mushrooms, bamboo shoot slices, carrots
and a few little pieces of pork. Sometimes a little spinach is
included.

57. TANUKI UDON　たぬきうどん　　　　　　　　Hot
▷　Soba-ya, Udon-ya

Noodles (specify SOBA or UDON) in a fish bouillon seasoned
with soy sauce. Small pieces of deep-fried (TEMPURA) flour
crusts are sprinkled over the top. Sometimes a little spinach or
a piece of fish cake may be added.

58. TEMPURA SOBA　天ぷらそば　　　　　　　　Hot
▷　Soba-ya, Udon-ya

A bowl of noodles (specify SOBA or UDON) in a fish bouillon
seasoned with soy sauce. One or two deep-fried shrimp TEM-
PURA are floating on the top. Sometimes a little spinach is
included.

59. TEN ZARU　天ざる　　　　　　　　　　　　　Cold
▷　Soba-ya, Udon-ya

Buckwheat noodles served on a bamboo rack in a laquered
box. (See listing No. 66, ZARU SOBA.) One or two deep-fried
shrimp TEMPURA and sometimes vegetables are arranged on
the side. Dip both the noodles and the TEMPURA into the soy
sauce broth before eating.

55. TA-MA-GO TO-JI

56. TAN-MEN

57. TA-NU-KI U-DON

58. TEM-PU-RA SO-BA

59. TEN-ZA-RU

35

60. TORORO SOBA とろろそば Hot

▷ Soba-ya, Udon-ya

Buckwheat noodles in fish bouillon seasoned with soy sauce. Covering the top of the soup is a thick, yellowish paste (TORO-RO) made from the root of the "YAMA-IMO." Thin strips of seaweed are often on the top. Leek slices and horseradish may be used as condiments. This dish is also called YAMA KAKE.

61. TSUKIMI SOBA 月見そば Hot

▷ Soba-ya, Udon-ya

Noodles (specify SOBA or UDON) in a fish bouillon seasoned with soy sauce. An egg set on a square of dried seaweed is placed on top of the noodles. (In Japanese this dish means "Autumn Moon Viewing" because the egg is seen as resembling the moon at autumn festival time.)

62. UDON SUKI......See No. 155

63. WANTAN ワンタン Hot

▷ Shokudō Chinese Restaurant

Wide noodle-like squares filled with a bit of ground pork and leeks served in a soy sauce seasoned soup. Sometimes a few vegetables, often spinach or Chinese bamboo pieces, are added on the top. With noodles this dish is called WANTAN MEN.

64. YAKI SOBA 焼きそば Hot

▷ Shokudō Street Stand Chinese Restauraut

There are two kinds of YAKI SOBA, YAWARAKAI (soft) and KATAI (crispy.) YAWARAKAI Y.S. is soft Chinese noodles fried on a griddle with small pieces of cabbage, carrots, pork, bean sprouts and sometimes squid pieces. KATAI Y.S. is crispy, dried Chinese noodles covered with a thick pork sauce containing small pieces of pork, Chinese cabbage, and sometimes carrots, onions, bamboo shoots, and pea pods.

65. YAMA-KAKE SOBA......See No. 60 TORORO SOBA

66. ZARU SOBA ざるそば Cold

▷ Soba-ya, Udon-ya

Boiled buckwheat noodles served cold on a bamboo rack in a lacquered box. A soy sauce seasoned dip comes in a small bottle on the side. Mix the few sliced leeks and dab of horseradish into the dip and eat the noodles a few at a time after putting them into this mixture.

67. ZĀSAI SOBA ザーサイそば Hot

▷ Chinese Restaurant Shokudō

Chinese noodles in a pork bouillon which. is flavored with ZASAI, Chinese pickles. A few pork pieces, bean sprouts and bamboo shoot slices are sometimes included.

60. TO-RO-RO SO-BA

61. TSU-KI-MI SO-BA

63. WAN-TAN

64. YA-WA-RA-KAI YA-KI-SO-BA

66. ZA-RU SO-BA

67. ZĀ-SA-I SO-BA

37

SUSHI YA . . . . . . The SUSHI Shop

Perhaps the most popular and distinctively Japanese of all foods is SUSHI (women use the polite "O-SUSHI"). It is so distinctive, in fact, that it is difficult to describe to one who has not tried it. SUSHI is made of the best grade of rice which has been delicately seasoned with vinegar, sugar and salt. The origins of SUSHI date back hundreds of years; at one point two distinct styles of SUSHI emerged, one in Edo (old Tokyo), the other in Osaka in the Kansai region. These two forms, NIGIRI ZUSHI (see Nos. 68–88) and OSHI ZUSHI (see No. 100) are characteristic of the two distinct styles of foods in these regions. Briefly, the difference is in the form as well as in the taste of the two kinds of SUSHI. The NIGIRI ZUSHI of the Tokyo region is shaped in the palm of the hand, resulting in small, oblong mounds of packed rice on which is placed the customer's choice of fresh (usually uncooked) fish. OSHI ZUSHI from Osaka is marinated or boiled fish and SUSHI rice pressed into a rectangular wooden mould, with the resulting block of rice cut into smaller sections for serving.

You can immediately identify the SUSHI Shop by looking at the containers in the wax model window displays. SUSHI is always served in laquered boxes or directly on the counter rather than on plates or in bowls.

SUSHI Shops are known for their genial chefs and friendly atmosphere. This feeling of welcome and warmth results not only from the engaging style of the SUSHI maker, but from the style of the shop as well. Most SUSHI shops are small with a single counter of clean, beautifully hewn, natural cedar. There are usually a few tables by a wall, but it's at the counter where the action is. Not only does a counter seat promise the best view of the extraordinary skills of the SUSHI maker, it is also the most convenient location for pointing to the kinds of SUSHI you will want to try. Moreover the best way to enjoy SUSHI is to have it served directly on the counter immediately as it is prepared for you. If all this is not enough to delight you, you might ponder how the SUSHI chef keeps track of who has eaten how many of which kinds of SUSHI without a bill.

The term "SUSHI" is a bit like the word "sandwich"; it refers to the base or style, but not to the important contents. And the variety of SUSHI, and fish available for SUSHI, is truly staggering, offering a range of fresh seafood that only the Japanese might take for granted. In addition to the varieties of SUSHI made with fish, there are many kinds which feature vegetables, seaweed and "omelets" topping or surrounding the rice. SUSHI, of course, is the feature of SUSHI Shops but one may also order SASHIMI (see No. 127), CHAWAN MUSHI (see No. 108) and occasionally loaches. Tea is served as a matter of course along with the damp, little towel, OSHIBORI, but beer and SAKE are popular complements to the SUSHI.

This description merely hints at the characteristic of SUSHI which so frightens some visitors to Japan who have heard of SUSHI but have never tried it: most of the seafood which tops SUSHI is raw. To the uninitiated, "raw fish" is an unnecessarily appalling prospect, but the reality, for most of us, is a delicious taste treat.

NIGIRI ZUSHI

Where you sit in the SUSHI Shop makes a difference.

If you sit at the counter it is generally understood that you intend to order NIGIRI ZUSHI, and that you will order each kind of fish individually. Two rice mounds with a slice of fish on top of each is considered one order. Perhaps the easiest way is to simply point out what you would like to try as the fish available are displayed in a refrigerated case attached to the counter directly in front of you. This method of ordering adds up to be more expensive than the standard combination plate, but it's more fun.

Kinds of Fish usually served as SUSHI:

(For a complete list of fish see Appendix Fish List.)

68. AKAGAI (raw) Ark shell, a reddish shell fish.
69. ANAGO (cooked) Conger eel, a long salt water fish served broiled and brushed with a thick sweet sauce.
70. AOYAGI (raw) Round clam, usually the reddish foot of the clam.
71. AWABI (raw) Abalone, a white slice with a brownish edge.
72. CHUTORO (raw) Tuna, light pinkish. a little fatty.
73. EBI (cooked) Shrimp, prawn.
74. HAMACHI (raw) A kind of mackerel.
75. HAMAGURI (raw) Clam.

76. **HIRAME** (raw) Flatfish, white with brownish coloring.
77. **IKA** (raw) Squid, cuttlefish, milky white sometimes served bound to the rice with seaweed.
78. **IKURA** (raw) Salmon or trout eggs.
79. **KOHADA** (marinated) A sardine-like fish, white with silvery gray skin dotted with black flecks.
80. **MAGURO NO AKAMI** (raw) Tuna fish, a reddish color (One of the favorites of foreigners who try SUSHI for the first time.)
81. **MIRUGAI** (boiled) A variety of round clam.
82. **SHAKO** (boiled) Mantis shrimp (gray color).
83. **SU-AJI** (marinated) Horse mackerel, light brownish with silver skin.
84. **TAIRAGAI** (raw) Round ligament.
85. **TAKO** (boiled) Octopus.
86. **TORIGAI** (boiled) A large shellfish.
87. **UNI** (raw) Orange eggs of the sea chestnut.
88. **NIGIRI ZUSHI** (a standard combination)

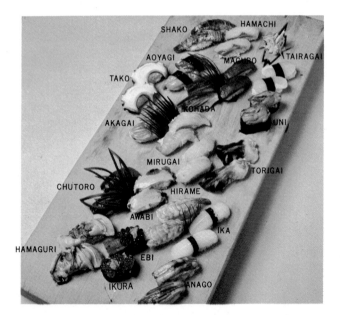

If you sit at a table you may order any kind of SUSHI including NIGIRI ZUSHI. If you order NIGIRI ZUSHI (see No. 88) you will not have the same freedom to select and eat a few at a time as does the customer at the counter. Instead you will be served a standard combination of several pairs of fish rice mounds artfully arranged. You may often specify the cheaper or the more expensive combination. "NAMI" —the cheaper assortment usually includes rice mounds topped with Tuna, Egg, Octopus, Conger eel, Squid, and a marinated Sardine-like fish.

"JO" —the more expensive assortment usually includes Abalone, Shrimp, Tuna, Sea Bream and eggs of the Sea Chestnut.

● SUSHI TERMS

MURASAKI (MU-RA-SA-KI) A special name for soy sauce which is usually known as **SHOYU**. MURASAKI is used only in SUSHI shops. It is the most familiar of the special vocabulary that goes with SUSHI eating.

WASABI (WA-SA-BI) Very spicy, green horseradish, sometimes made from freshly grated roots, but usually made from powdered, canned horseradish. Some of this spice is automatically included under the fish slice of each NIGIRI ZUSHI, or as a little green dab meant to be mixed into soy sauce and eaten with SASHIMI and other dishes.

If you don't want any horseradish say "SABINUKI" (SA-BI-NU-KI). This is a good word to use if you don't like any spicy foods or if you are ordering for children.

If you want only a little horseradish (or anything else) say "SUKOSHI" (SU-KO-SHI).

90. CHI-RA-SHI ZU-SHI

CHA-KIN ZU-SHI

89. CHAKIN ZUSHI 茶巾ずし   Cold

Seasoned rice wrapped beautifully with a thin, yellow egg crepe. Sometimes the top is folded over and tied and sometimes it is arranged in a ruffle with a single pea and a small shrimp decorating the center. This dish is also called FUKUSA ZUSHI.

90. CHIRASHI ZUSHI ちらしずし   Cold

A bowl of seasoned rice covered with slices of many different kinds of raw or marinated fish. NORI and pickled ginger are under the fish (in the Kyōto-Ōsaka area they are mixed into the rice). The fish combination depends on the price. You can specify: NAMI (or UME) – the cheapest combination, JŌ (or TAKE) – the middle priced combination, TOKU (or MATSU) – the most expensive combination.

91. DATE MAKI . . . . . . See No. 102 TAMAGO MAKI

92. FUKUSA ZUSHI . . . . . . See No. 89 CHAKIN ZUSHI

● **SUSHI TERMS**

AGARI (A-GA-RI) The term used in SUSHI shops to mean a large cup of green tea. AGARI means literally "to complete." There is no charge for this tea and you may have as many cups as you like.

GARI (GA-RI) The fresh, pickled ginger slices (light pink) usually called SUSHOGA are called GARI in SUSHI restaurants. An unlimited quantity of these are available to be eaten with SUSHI.

42

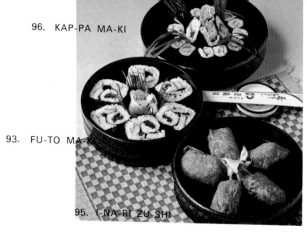

96. KAP-PA MA-KI

93. FU-TO MA-KI

95. I-NA-RI ZU-SHI

Cold

93. FUTO MAKI　太巻きずし

A colorful slice made from a long roll of seasoned rice wrapped with NORI with egg, bits of vegetables, mushrooms, KAMPYO and fish powder in the center. This dish is also called NORI MAKI in Osaka-Kyoto area.

94. HAKO ZUSHI......See No. 100 OSHI ZUSHI

95. INARI ZUSHI　いなりずし
Cold

Seasoned rice stuffed into a bag made of fried TŌFU called ABURAGE which has been boiled in a sweet sauce. (Children frequently like these.) INARI ZUSHI cannot be ordered in the Sushi Shop, but is a common street stand food.

96. KAPPA MAKI　かっぱ巻き
Cold

Small rolls of seasoned rice cut from a long seaweed-covered roll with a piece of fresh cucumber and a little horseradish in the center. The KAPPA, an imaginary river creature, is thought to like cucumbers which he steals from fields near the banks of rivers.

97. NIGIRI ZUSHI......See　Pages 39–41

98. NORI MAKI　のり巻き
Cold

Seasoned rice rolled in seaweed. A long strip of sweet KAMPYŌ is in the center.

In Ōsaka and Kyōto, this name is used for the SUSHI described as FUTO MAKI. See No. 93.

99. OSHINKO MAKI　おしんこ巻き
Cold

Seasoned rice rolled in seaweed. A piece of yellow, pickled radish is in the center.

100. O-SHI ZU-SHI

98. NO-RI MA-KI

99. O-SHIN-KO MA-KI

100. OSHI ZUSHI　押しずし　　　　　　Cold
Ōsaka style SUSHI

A general term for the kind of SUSHI which developed in Ōsaka. (See SUSHI introduction.) Pressed seasoned rice with cooked fish or egg on top and cut into squares.

101. SABA ZUSHI　さばずし　　　　　　Cold
Ōsaka style SUSHI

Seasoned rice mounds topped with marinated mackerel slices. (Called BATTERA in Kyōto-Ōsaka area.)

102. TAMAGO MAKI　卵巻き　　　　　　Cold

Seasoned rice wrapped in a thick slice of egg omelet. Bits of mushroom, KAMPYO, NORI and green vegetables are arranged inside. This colorful slice is also called DATE MAKI.

103. TEKKA MAKI　てっか巻き　　　　　　Cold

Seasoned rice rolled in seaweed with a piece of raw tuna fish and a bit of horseradish inside. Many small rolls are arranged in the lacquered box.

102. TA-MA-GO MA-KI

103. TEK-KA MA-KI

101. SA-BA ZU-SHI

44

104. TEKKA DONBURI

てっかどんぶり　　Cold

Seasoned rice with many slices of raw tuna on the top. A few squares of dried seaweed are hiding under the tuna. A dab of horse-radish and pickled ginger slices are in the center or are sometimes underneath the tuna.

104.
TEK-KA DON-BU-RI

A LA CARTE DISHES

105. AJI TATAKI　あじのたたき　　　　　　Cold

▷　Koryōri-ya　Kyōdo Ryori

A kind of SASHIMI. Small pieces of raw pompano fish chopped and mixed with onion, ginger and sometimes leeks. This dish is elegantly served as a graceful whole fish resting on curled slivers of radish or seaweed. The middle section pieces are arranged between the whole head and tail. A dip of soy sauce, ginger and the buds and flowers of the HOJISO plant is usually included.

106. BATA YAKI　バター焼き　　　　　　Hot

▷　Meshi-ya　Specialty Restaurant

Thinly sliced beef, sometimes pork, fried in butter and seasoned with salt. Some vegetables may be included.

105. A-JI TA-TA-KI

106. BA-TA YA-KI

45

107. BUTA SHŌGA YAKI　豚しょうが焼き　　　Hot
　　▷　Specialty Restaurant　Shokuji Dokoro

Pork slices marinated beforehand and then cooked in the same sauce which is made from soy sauce and freshly grated ginger. More expensive servings may include a vegetable salad on the side.

108. CHAWAN MUSHI　茶わん蒸し　　　Hot
　　▷　Sushi-ya　Koryōri-ya

A delicious dinner custard (poached soup) made from a fish broth and eggs. Pieces of chicken, shrimp, fish cakes, a mushroom, ginko nuts and pea pods are usually in the custard. A trefoil leaf often decorates the top.

109. CHIRI MUSHI　ちり蒸し　　　Hot
　　▷　Koryōri-ya　Kappō

A piece of fish filet and a few vegetables steamed in a medium sized bowl and served as one course of a multi-course meal. The fish is usually tilefish or sea bream and the vegetables frequently include a mushroom, TŌFU, ginko nuts and a bit of spinach. A tiny citron peel adds flavor. A sauce dip using lemon, grated radish, leeks and soy sauce is served in a side dish.

110. DASHI MAKI......See No. 133 TAMAGO YAKI

111. DENGAKU　でんがく　　　Hot
　　▷　Nomi-ya　Koryōri-ya　Festival Food

Rectangles of TŌFU, or KONNYAKU skewered on bamboo sticks. The TŌFU has been covered with a MISO sauce and broiled over charcoal. Edible KONOME leaves decorate the top. The name is taken from a form of ancient folk drama, DENGAKU. Sometimes eggplant, radish or potato is served this way minus the skewers.

112. DOBIN MUSHI　どびん蒸し　　　Hot
　　▷　Kappō　Koryōri-ya

Whole or sliced mushrooms (MATSUTAKE), bits of chicken (sometimes shrimp), ginko nuts and a few vegetables in a soup made from fish bouillon seasoned with SAKE and sweet wine. This dish is served in a small, earthen teapot the lid or a separate saucer should be used as your plate. Lemon or citron juice is used as a spice. This attractive dish is an autumn favorite as these special mushrooms are abundant in the fall.

113. EDAMAME　枝豆　　　Cold
　　▷　Nomi-ya　Koryōri-ya

Boiled, green soy beans served as an appetizer in their salted pods. Only the beans inside are to be eaten.

107. BU-TA SHŌ-GA YA-KI

108. CHA-WAN MU-SHI

109. CHI-RI MU-SHI

111. DEN-GA-KU

112. DO-BIN MU-SHI

113. E-DA-MA-ME

47

114. HIMONO 干物   Hot
   ▷ Nomi-ya

An hors d'oeuvre: broiled, dried fish which has sometimes been cut in half and salted. Horse mackerel, pike, sardine, and small flatfish are often used. Some grated radish is often used as a condiment.

115. HIYA YAKKO 冷ややっこ   Cold
   ▷ Nomi-ya Koryōri-ya

One cube of cold TOFU (bean curd) served with chopped leeks and grated ginger. Soy sauce should be poured over the top or mixed with the spices in a separate dish to be used as a seasoning. Sometimes SANSHO leaves are used to decorate the top. These, too, are meant to be eaten.

116. IKA SHŌGA YAKI いかしょうが焼き   Hot
   ▷ Nomi-ya

Squid pieces grilled with a seasoning of soy sauce, grated ginger and garlic.

117. ITAWASA 板わさ   Cold
   ▷ Nomi-ya Koryōri-ya

Several slices of white fish cake (KAMABOKO) arranged in a row to be eaten as an appetizer. A bit of horseradish and soy sauce should be mixed together and used as a dip.

118. KAKI AGE かき揚げ   Hot
   ▷ Tempura-ya Shokuji Dokoro

A deep fried TEMPURA circle of small vegetables and pork or shrimp pieces. (It is the cheapest kind of TEMPURA.) Dip the KAKIAGE into the soup-like sauce provided on the side. A bowl of rice can be ordered separately.

119. KIMPIRA きんぴら
   ▷ Kyodo Ryori Cold
       Nomi-ya

Fried burdock root and carrot strips seasoned with soy sauce, sugar and red pepper.

120. MISOSHIRU みそ汁
   ▷ Meshi-ya   Hot
       Koryōri-ya
       Shokuji Dokoro
       Tempura-ya

A very popular soup often eaten for breakfast or as one course of a multi-course meal.

120. MI-SO-SHI-RU

114. HI-MO-NO

115. HI-YA YAK-KO

116. I-KA SHŌ-GA YA-KI

117. I-TA-WA-SA

118. KA-KI A-GE

119. KIN-PI-RA

49

There are many ways to make it, however the base is always DASHI (fish or seaweed bouillon) seasoned with MISO (fermented bean paste). Small squares of TOFU and soft seaweed or other vegetables are also used in the soup.

121. NAMA YASAI 生野菜 Cold
▷ Koryōri-ya Nomi-ya Shokuji Dokoro

Fresh vegetable salad usually containing a little lettuce, cucumber, tomato, onion slices and a section of hard boiled egg. Sometimes asparagus and a little red cabbage are also included.

122. NATTŌ 納豆 Cold
▷ Nomi-ya Shokuji Dokoro

Fermented soy beans in a brownish, sticky paste seasoned with soy sauce and leek slices. It is usually eaten with rice. When served as an hors d'oeuvre dried seaweed and a raw quail egg are sometimes on the top. Sold in the store, NATTŌ comes in an interesting straw package. The taste resembles a strong cheese.

123. ODEN おでん Hot
▷ Oden-ya Nomi-ya Koryōri-ya Street and Festival Food

A variety of many pressed fish cakes, TOFU cubes, sliced radish, hard boiled egg, KONNYAKU seaweed and sometimes octopus boiled together in a large pot of fish bouillon. Usually a standard plate combination will be served with a dab of hot mustard on the side. But sometimes each piece is individually skewered and you can point out piece by piece the ones you would like to try. The name comes from a form of ancient folk drama. The skewered TOFU was seen as resembling the person on stilts in the play.

124. OHITASHI おひたし Cold
▷ Koryōri-ya Nomi-ya

Boiled spinach or other green vegetable served in a small bowl. It is seasoned with soy sauce and sesame seeds or shaved dried bonito. (In Tokyo OHITASHI sounds like "OSHITASHI")

125. SAKANA TERIYAKI 魚照り焼き Hot
▷ Koryōri-ya Nomi-ya

A piece of fish filet, usually yellowtail or mackerel, broiled with soy sauce, SAKE, sugar and MIRIN. It is sometimes served with an edible stalk of fresh pickled ginger.

126. SANSAI NITSUKE 山菜煮つけ Cold
▷ Nomi-ya Koryōri-ya Onigiri-ya Kyōdo Ryōri

A small dish of seasonal, mountain flowering fern which has been boiled in fish bouillon seasoned with soy sauce and sweet wine. It is often served with SAKE as an hors d'oeuvre.

121. NA-MA YA-SA-I

122. NAT-TŌ

123. O-DEN

124. O-HI-TA-SHI

125. SA-KA-NA TE-RI-YA-KI

126. SA-N-SA-I NI-TSU-KE

51

127. SASHIMI さしみ　　　　　　　　　　　　Cold
128. SASHIMI TEISHOKU さしみ定食
　　▷　Kappō　Shokuji Dokoro

The name for any one (or a combination) of a variety of very
fresh pieces of raw fish (see Appendix Fish List) artfully arranged on a special, flat dish or wooden platter. It is usually eaten
as an hors d'oeuvre or as one course of a meal. However, it
can be the main course when ordered as SASHIMI TEISHOKU.
TEISHOKU means a complete meal including soup, rice,
pickles, and sometimes another dish. An order of SASHIMI
(polite O-SASHIMI) for two or more people will be served on
a single plate.

The SASHIMI of sea bream (TAI) is generally regarded by the
Japanese as the most delicious, although the people of Tokyo
consider tuna (MAGURO) the best.

To stimulate the appetite, SASHIMI must be arranged artis-
tically hence the fish slices are always accompanied by decorative
raw vegetables called TSUMA. These are also meant to be
eaten.

129. SAZAE TSUBOYAKI さざえのつぼ焼き　　　Hot
　　▷　Nomi-ya　Koryōri-ya　Kyōdo Ryōri

A single, spiral shaped shellfish (wreath shell) often served
elegantly on a bed of salt. The meat has usually been chopped,
replaced in its shell and boiled in a little soy sauce and SAKE.
Trefoil may be used as a seasoning.

130. SHIO YAKI 塩焼き　　　　　　　　　　　Hot
　　▷　Kappō　Koryōri-ya　Nomi-ya　Shokuji Dokoro

A small, whole fish coated with salt and broiled until the skin
is crisp. The fish is usually AYU (Japanese river trout), TAI
(sea bream) or KAMASU (pike).

131. SUIMONO 吸い物　　　　　　　　　　　　Hot
　　▷　Koryōri-ya　Shokuji Dokoro　Nomi-ya　Kappō

A general term for any clear soup usually made from fish
bouillon or seaweed, soy sauce, SAKE and salt. A few boiled
vegetables (often trefoil, a fish cake and a mushroom) are
artfully cut and served in the soup. A tiny slice of citron peel
is frequently added for flavor. Good SUIMONO is a test of
a good cook as it requires experience and skill.

132. SUNOMONO 酢の物　　　　　　　　　　　Cold
　　▷　Koryōri-ya　Shokuji Dokoro　Kappō

A very small serving of salted fresh vegetables mixed with small
pieces of raw fish and seasoned with sugar and vinegar. Soft
seaweed, WAKAME, is sometimes used as the vegetable.

127. SA-SHI-MI

128. SA-SHI-MI TEI-SHO-KU

129. SA-ZA-E TSU-BO-YA-KI

130. SHI-O YA-KI

131. SU-I-MO-NO

132. SU-NO-MO-NO

53

133. TAMAGO YAKI　卵焼き　　　　　　　Hot
▷　Koryōri-ya　Shokuji-Dokoro

A kind of omelet; eggs cooked in layers with soy sauce and sweet wine seasoning and then served in two thick slices. Sometimes a maple leaf or other leaf is used for decoration. (These are not edible although the stalk of pickled ginger is.) Sometimes grated radish mixed with soy sauce is used as a dip. This dish is also called DASHI MAKI.

134. TATSUTA AGE.. See No. 137 TORI KARA AGE　Hot
▷　Koryōri-ya　Shokuji Dokoro　Nomi-ya

Chunks of chicken (or sometimes fish filet) which have been marinated in soy sauce and SAKE and then fried.

135. TEMPURA......See No. 15.

136. TON KATSU　トンカツ　　　　　　　Hot
▷　Shokudō　Shokuji Dokoro　Yōshoku-ya　Tonkatsu-ya

Breaded pork cutlet, deep fried and served on a plate with a mound of shredded cabbage and/or a little potato salad (sometimes macaroni salad). A few tomato wedges, orange slices or a bit of cucumber are usually included. A large serving of rice, (RA-I-SU), is sometimes served on the same plate or separately, (TON KATSU RAISU). Frequently you can specify which cut of meat you prefer:

RŌSU—the standard pork cutlet
HIRE—more expensive pork filet
HITO KUCHI KATSU—lean chunks of pork

137. TORI KARA AGE　鶏から揚げ　　　　　Hot
▷　Koryōri-ya　Nomi-ya

Chunks of deep fried chicken seasoned with salt. Some fried vegetables and a piece of lemon may be included. (TATSUTA AGE looks the same, but the chicken has been marinated in soy sauce and SAKE before being fried.)

138. UNAJŪ......See No. 21.

139. USU ZUKURI　薄作り　　　　　　　Cold
▷　Kappō　Specialty Restaurant

Thinly sliced raw fish arranged in the shape of a flower. (Blowfish, Snapping Turtle or Flounder are often used.) A side dish containing leek slices, grated radish, citron juice, soy sauce and DASHI is to be used as a dip. This dish is almost always rather expensive.

140. YAKI TORI　焼き鳥　　　　　　　Hot
▷　Nomi-ya Yakitori-ya　Street Stand　Koryōri-ya

Small pieces of chicken or chicken liver (and sometimes pieces of leek) are arranged on bamboo skewers and grilled over char-

133. TA-MA-GO YA-KI

136. TON KA-TSU

137. TO-RI KA-RA A-GE

139. U-SU ZU-KU-RI

coal. Just bofore serving they
are dipped into a kind of
barbecue sauce. When ordered
at a street stand you should
specify the number of skewers
you want:

1—IPPON
2—NIHON
3—SANBON
4—YONHON
5—GOHON
6—ROPPON

140. YA-KI TO-RI

141. YAKI HAMAGURI　焼きはまぐり　　　　　Hot
　　　▷　Kappō　Koryōri-ya　Nomiya

A few broiled clams served in the shell on a bed of salt with a slice of lemon.

142. YAKI NIKU　焼き肉　　　　　　　　　　Hot
　　　▷　Shokudō　Nomi-ya

Fried, thinly sliced pork which has been marinated in soy sauce, sugar, ginger and garlic. A few vegetables may or may not be included.

143. YANAGAWA NABE　柳川なべ　　　　　　Hot
　　　▷　Unagi-ya　Shokuji Dokoro

Loaches and sliced burdock root covered with egg cooked in a sweetened soy sauce. This food is cooked in a special crockery dish, which is placed on a lacquer stand when served.

144. YASAI NITSUKE　野菜煮つけ　　　　　　Cold
　　　▷　Koryōri-ya　Nomiya

A small bowl of cooked seasonal Japanese vegetables, often taro root, pea pods, KONNYAKU and carrots which have been cooked with soy sauce, salt and sugar. Sometimes bamboo shoots and lotus roots are the vegetables used.

145. YUDŌFU　湯どうふ　　　　　　　　　　Hot
　　　▷　Koryōri-ya　Nomiya

Small squares of TOFU boiled in an earthen ware pot (sometimes at your table). Eat the pieces after dipping them into a sauce made with leeks, ginger, shaved dried bonito and soy sauce.

146. ZŌNI　ぞう煮　　　　　　　　　　　　Hot
　　　▷　Sunakku　Kissaten　Kanmi-ya

A soup containing 1 or 2 rice cakes (MOCHI), a mushroom, a small piece of chicken, a fish cake slice and seasoned with citron peel and trefoil leaves. This is the special soup used to celebrate the New Year in almost all Japanese households. Traditionally ZŌNI (polite O-ZŌNI) is eaten just after drinking the spicy New Year's SAKE on the morning of January 1st and then on each of following two day of the New Year holidays. In Osaka and Kyoto the soup is made with MISO paste. During any time of the year ZŌNI is available as a light snack in traditional Japanese dessert shops.

147. ZŌSUI......See No. 24.

141. YA-KI HA-MA-GU-RI

142. YA-KI NI-KU

143. YA-NA-GA-WA NA-BE

144. YA-SA-I NI-TSU-KE

145. YU-DŌ-FU

146. ZŌ-NI

57

DISHES PREPARED AT THE TABLE

148. CHIRI NABE　ちりなべ　　　　　　　　Hot

▷　Koryōri-ya　　Nomi-ya

Fish, usually cod fish, blowfish or angler, boiled with leeks, cabbage, mushrooms and TOFU in an earthen ware pot cooked at your table. A spicy CHIRIZU sauce is served as a dip.

148.
CHI-RI-NA-BE

149. DOTE NABE　土手なべ　　　　　　　　Hot

▷　Koryōri-ya　　Specialty Restaurant

Oysters, leeks and edible chrysanthemum leaves are cooked in a pottery casserole which is lined with sweet MISO paste. A raw egg is served in an individual dish to be used as a dip. (Winter season only.)

149.　DO-TE NA-BE

150. MIZUTAKI　水たき　　　　　Hot

▷　Koryōri-ya　Specialty Restaurant

Chicken pieces, Chinese cabbage, leeks, TOFU and vermicelli are served on a large plate. An earthen pot containing a stock made from seaweed or dried fish shavings is set to boil in the center of your table. Cook the chicken and vegetables a few at a time and eat them as they are ready. A spicy sauce to be used as a dip is served to each person.

151. OKONOMI YAKI　お好み焼き　　　　Hot

▷　Specialty Restaurant　Festival Food　Street Stand

A kind of thick, spicy pancake made from a batter containing chopped vegetables and the customer's choice of meat or seafood, usually chicken, beef, shrimp, squid or egg. The cheapest kinds are thin, often made with an egg broken and merely sprinkled with several spices or a bit of vegetables and fish. The more expensive kinds are thick and filling.

151. O-KO-NO-MI YA-KI

152. SHA-BU SHA-BU

152. SHABU SHABU　しゃぶしゃぶ　　　　　Hot

▷　Specialty Restaurant　Kappō

Slices of tender beef and various vegetables, usually Chinese cabbage, TOFU, and leeks are served on a large platter. An unusual copper or brass pot with a chimney in the center is placed on the table. Each guest boils a portion of the beef and vegetables in the stock on his side of the pot. A special dip of MISO, sesame seeds, soy sauce, or of lemon juice and grated radish is served to each guest. (This dish is always rather expensive because of the use of beef.)

153. SUKIYAKI　すき焼き　　　　　　　Hot

▷　Specialty Restaurant

Thin slices of beef (sometimes chicken) cooked in a special iron pan with various vegetables, usually leeks, mushrooms, TOFU,

Chinese cabbage, and vermicelli. The vegetables and meat are boiled in a small quantity of stock made from SAKE, sugar, soy sauce and DASHI. This dish is usually eaten with rice, and a raw egg dip is used for the foods taken from the common pot.

153. SU-KI-YA-KI

154. TEP-PAN YA-KI

154. TEPPAN YAKI　鉄板焼き　　　　　Hot

▷ Sunakku　Koryōri-ya

Thinly sliced beef or pork is cooked on a grill at your table with a few vegetables: onions, green peppers, bean sprouts and mushrooms. In more expensive varieties shellfish are included and the beef is the thickness of steak. Rice can be ordered separately.

155. UDON SUKI　うどんすき　　　　　Hot

▷ Soba-ya, Udon-ya　Specialty Restaurant

Chicken and sometimes shrimp or clams and white noodles boiled in a SUKIYAKI sauce with leeks mushrooms and edible chrysanthemum leaves.

155. U-DON SU-KI

CHINESE DISHES

156. ANMAN......See No. 171 MANTŌ.

157. BUTA PĪMAN ITAME 豚ピーマンいため　　　Hot
　　▷　Chinese Restaurant

Fried pork pieces mixed with green peppers and sometimes carrots and onions covered with a thick sauce.

158. CHĀHAN......See No. 1.

159. CHANPON......See No. 26.

160. CHŪKA DONBURI......See No. 2.

161. EBI KARASHI ITAME エビからしいため　　　Hot
　　▷　Chinese Restaurant

Spicy, fried shrimp mixed with a thick sweet sauce made from ginger, red pepper, onion, garlic, SAKE and soy sauce. Sometimes peas are added for color.

162. GOMOKU SOBA......See No. 30.

163. GYŌZA ギョーザ　　　Hot
　　▷　Shokudō　Chinese Restaurant　Street Stand

Fried and steamed crescent shaped Chinese pastry stuffed with a mixture of chives, Chinese cabbage and ground pork served in a row on a plate. You can make your own dip of sesame seed oil, vinegar and hot pepper. (Containers are on the table.)

164. HAPPŌ SAI 八宝菜　　　Hot
　　▷　Chinese Restaurant

Fried pork pieces with mushrooms, bamboo shoots, carrots, pea pods, onions, water chestnuts mixed with a thick bouillon seasoned with sesame seed oil, soy sauce, sugar and salt.

165. HARU MAKI 春巻き　　　Hot
　　▷　Chinese Restaurant

Chinese Egg Roll called in Japanese "Spring Roll." Deep fried pastry filled with vegetables and ground pork (or shrimp.) You can make your own dip of oil, vinegar, mustard and soy sauce.

157. BU-TA PĪ-MAN I-TA-ME

161. E-BI KA-RA-SHI I-TA-ME

163. GYŌ-ZA

164. HAP-PŌ SA-I

165. HA-RU MA-KI

166. KANI TAMA　かに玉　　　　　　　　　Hot

▷ Chinese Restauraut

An egg omelet filled with crab, leek slices, bamboo shoot slices, and mushroom slices. The omelet is sometimes covered with a thick sauce seasoned with sugar and soy sauce.

167. KANTON MEN......See No. 38.

168. KOI MARUAGE　こいのまる揚げ　　　　Hot

▷ Chinese Restauraut

Deep fried whole carp (very crispy, head and most bones are edible) covered with a thick tomato sauce containing bamboo shoots, mushrooms, carrots and sometimes pork pieces.

169. KURAGE SUNOMONO　くらげの酢の物　　Cold

▷ Chinese Restaurant

Sliced, parboiled and jellyfish usually mixed with cucumber strips and a sauce made from sugar, vinegar, sesame oil, pepper and soy sauce.

170. MABŌ TOFU　麻婆豆腐　　　　　　　　Hot

▷ Chinese Restaurant

Small squares of TOFU in a soupy mixture containing ground pork seasoned with leeks, ginger, sesame seed oil and soy sauce. Sometimes very spicy.

171. MANTŌ　マントウ　　　　　　　　　　Hot

NIKU-MAN......Meat filling
AN-MAN......Sweet bean paste filling

▷ Chinese Restaurant Street Stand

A Chinese wheat dumpling (a steamed white bun) filled with a little ground pork and vegetable mixture (NIKU MAN) or some sweet bean paste (AN MAN).

172. MOYASHI SOBA......See No. 46

173. NIKU DANGO　肉だんご　　　　　　　Hot

▷ Chinese Restaurant

Meat balls made from ground pork, ginger and leeks sometimes covered with a thick sweet-sour sauce. Cheaper versions have only 5 or 6 meat balls and always include the sauce.

166. KA-NI TA-MA

168. KO-I MA-RU-A-GE

169. KU-RA-GE SU-NO-MO-NO

170. MÃ-BŌ TŌ-FU

171. MAN-TŌ

173. NI-KU DAN-GO

65

174. NIKUMAN......See No. 171. MANTŌ

175. NIKU KARA-AGE 肉から揚げ　　　　　　Hot
▷ Chinese Restaurant

Deep fried pieces of meat, usually pork (BUTA-KARA-AGE) or chicken (TORI-KARA-AGE). The pieces are seasoned with soy sauce and SAKE and fried in a batter of potato starch. Sometimes a bit of parsley or sliced leek and a little mound of salt and pepper are included on the plate as condiments.

176. NIKU MISO SOBA 肉みそそば　　　　　Cold
▷ Chinese Restaurant

Chinese noodles (no soup) in a bowl covered with a spicy sauce made from MISO, ground pork, bamboo shoots and mushrooms. Fresh cucumber strips are usually served next to the sauce.

177. NIRA REBĀ ITAME にらレバーいため　　Hot
▷ Meshi-ya　Shokudō　Chinese Restaurant

Pork liver slices sautéed with spring onion leaves, bean sprouts and sometimes carrots and seasoned with soy sauce, salt and SAKE.

178. SHŪMAI シューマイ　　　　　　　　Hot
▷ Shokudō　Chinese Restaurant　Street Stand

Small steamed pork meat balls wrapped in a thin pastry usually decorated with a single pea on top. (Very common.)

179. SUBUTA 酢豚　　　　　　　　　　　Hot
▷ Chinese Restaurant

Fried pieces of pork mixed with a thick soy sauce and vinegar seasoned sauce containing onions, carrots, bamboo shoots and sometimes pineapple. (Looks like sweet & sour pork, but the sauce is different.) Rice, "RAISU", must be ordered separately.

180. SUI GYŌZA 水ぎょうざ　　　　　　　Hot
▷ Chinese Restaurant

Chinese crescent shaped pastries stuffed with a chive, cabbage and pork mixture served floating in a pork bouillon seasoned with leek slices. This is served with a bit of peppered sesame oil, or you can make your own dip from the condiments on the table. A little spinach may be included.

175. NI-KU KA-RA-A-GE

176. NI-KU MI-SO SO-BA

177. NI-RA RE-BĀ I-TA-ME

178. SHŪ-MA-I

179. SU-BU-TA

180. SU-I GYŌZA

181. TAMAGO SŪPU　卵のスープ　　　　Hot

▷　Shokudō　Chinese Restauraut

A clear pork seasoned soup with egg, bits of leek and KIKU-RAGE mixed in.

182. TENSHIN DONBURI　天津どん　　　Hot

▷　Chinese Restaurant

Rice covered by an egg omelet made with crab, onions and peas. A thick soy sauce gravy covers the top. This dish is sometimes called "TENSHIN HAN."

183. TENSHIN MEN　天津めん　　　　Hot

▷　Chinese Restaurant

Chinese noodles in a soy flavored bouillon. An egg omelet containing crab, onions and peas—is on top. Sometimes a thick sauce is poured over the omelet.

184. TORI KARA-AGE......See No. 175. NIKU KARA-AGE

185. TORI KASHŪ ITAME　鶏カシューいため　　Hot

▷　Chinese Restaurant

Pieces of fried chicken and cashew (KASHŪ) nuts, sometimes peanuts (PĪNATSU), mixed together in a thick sauce made from ginger, SAKE and soy sauce. The photo shows PĪNATSU-ITAME.

186. WANTAN......See No. 63.

187. YASAI ITAME　野菜いため　　　　Hot

▷　Shokudō　Chinese Restaurant

A variety of vegetables fried together usually with carrots, cabbage, mushrooms, green peppers and bean sprouts or bamboo shoot.

188. YASAI SŪPU　野菜スープ　　　　Hot

▷　Shokudō　Chinese Restaurant

A pork-flavored vegetable soup, containing pieces of carrots, bamboo shoots, mushrooms and cabbage.

189. ZĀSAI SOBA......See No. 67.

181. TA-MA-GO SŪ-PU

182. TEN-SHIN DON-BU-RI

183. TEN-SHIN MEN

185. TO-RI KA-SHŪ I-TA-ME

187. YA-SA-I I-TA-ME

188. YA-SA-I SŪ-PU

69

190　　　191　　　192　　　193

DESSERTS

190. ABEKAWA MOCHI あべかわもち　　　Cold
(A-BE-KA-WA MO-CHI)
▷　Kanmi-ya Kissaten

Usually 3 rice cakes (MOCHI) covered with a yellow, slightly sweet bean powder.

191. ANMITSU あんみつ　　　Cold
(AN-MI-TSU)
▷　Kissaten Tea Room Kanmi-ya

The most popular traditional Japanese dessert. Whitish, gelatin cubes made from seaweed extract served with a scoop of sweet, brown bean paste and a few pieces of fruit. A small container of honey or syrup will be served with this dish to be used as a topping.

192. FURŪTSU MITSUMAME フルーツみつ豆　　　Cold
(FU-RŪ-TSU MI-TSU-MA-ME)
▷　Kanmi-ya Tea Room Kissaten

A few pieces of fruit served on top of gelatin cubes made from seaweed extract. Some whole, sweet beans are mixed among the gelatin cubes, and a few small pieces of colored rice candy (GYŪHI) are usually on the side. A little honey or syrup is to be used as a topping.

193. ISO MAKI いそ巻き　　　Cold
(I-SO MA-KI)
▷　Kanmi-ya Kissaten

Three grilled rice cakes (MOCHI) seasoned with soy sauce. A piece of dried seaweed is wrapped around each cake.

70

194. KŌRI AZUKI 氷あずき Cold
(KŌ-RI A-ZU-KI)

▷ Kissaten Shokudō Soba-ya, Udon-ya Kanmi-ya

A mound of shaved ice covered with sweet syrup. A scoop of brown sweet bean paste is hiding on the bottom and sometimes a dab of this bean jam is added to the top.

195. KŌRI ICHIGO ....Shaved ice with strawberry syrup.

196. KŌRI MERON ....Shaved ice with green, melon flavored syrup.

197. KŌRI MIRUKU....Shaved ice with sweetened condensed milk.

198. KŌRI REMON ......Shaved ice with lemon syrup.

199. KURĪMU ANMITSU クリームあんみつ Cold
(KU-RĪ-MU AN-MI-TSU)

▷ Kissaten Tea Room Kanmi-ya

A scoop of vanilla ice cream on top of gelatin cubes made from seaweed extract. Some sweet bean paste and a few pieces of fruit are also included. Honey or syrup is served in a small container to be used as a topping.

200. KURĪMU MITSUMAME クリームみつ豆 Cold
(KŪ-RĪ-MU MI-TSU-MA-ME)

▷ Kissaten Tea Room Kanmi-ya

Gelatin cubes made from seaweed extract mixed with some whole, sweet beans. A scoop of vanilla ice cream and a few fruit pieces are on the top.

71

201. KUZU MOCHI　くずもち　　　Cold

(KU-ZU MO-CHI)

▷ Kanmi-ya　Kissaten

Several triangular-shaped cakes made from arrowroot and covered with brown sugar syrup sprinkled with yellow bean powder.

202. MITSUMAME　みつ豆　　　Cold

(MI-TSU-MA-ME)

▷ Kissaten　Tea Room　Kanmi-ya

One of the most popular traditional Japanese desserts. Cubes of gelatin made from seaweed extract mixed with some whole, sweet beans. A few pieces of fruit are usually on the top. Honey or syrup is served separately to be used as a topping.

203. PURIN　プリン　　　Cold

(PU-RIN)

▷ Kissaten　Tea Room　Shokudō

A small vanilla-egg custard with a little brown sugar baked into the bottom. Sometimes a few pieces of fruit and a little whipped cream are added. Pudding.

204. SHIRUKO　しるこ　　　Hot

(SHI-RU-KO)

▷ Shiruko-ya　Kanmi-ya　Kissaten

A dark, sweet bean paste soup with pieces of rice cake (MOCHI) in it. Sometimes a small dish of pickles is served to complement the sweet taste of this dish. (Polite O-SHIRUKO.)

205. UJI GŌRI　宇治氷　　　　　　　Cold

(U-JI GŌ-RI)

▷　Kissaten　Shokudō　Soba-ya, Udon-ya　Kanmi-ya

Shaved ice with Japanese green tea syrup poured over the top.

206. UJI KINTOKI　宇治金時　　　　　Cold

(U-JI KIN-TO-KI)

▷　Kissaten　Shokudō　Soba-ya, Udon-ya　Kanmi-ya

A layer of sweet bean paste under a mound of shaved ice covered with green tea syrup. Sometimes a bit of bean paste is used to decorate the top.

207. TOKOROTEN　ところてん　　　　Cold

(TO-KO-RO-TEN)

▷　Kanmi-ya　Kissaten

Noodle-like strips of gelatin made from seaweed extract served in a tangy soy sauce. Pieces of dried seaweed decorate the top. Grated ginger may be used as a spice.

208. ZENZAI　ぜんざい　　　　　　　Hot

(ZEN-ZA-I)

▷　Kanmi-ya　Kissaten

A thick, sweet bean jam containing many whole beans and two rice cakes (MOCHI).

209. Numbers 209, 210, 211, 212, 213 labels under images.

209. AISU KŌHĪ Iced coffee, almost always pre-sweetened.

210. GURĒPU JŪSU Grape juice drink (carbonated.)

211. ICHIGO JŪSU A strawberry drink made from a sweet syrup.

212. KŌCHA Black tea. Usually served already brewed in a cup with a lemon slice.

213. KŌHĪ Coffee. (One cup, no refills. If you want more you must order a new cup.)

214. KOKOA Cocoa. **215. KŌRA** Any cola.

216. KŌRA FURŌTO Cola float. One scoop of vanilla ice-cream in any kind of cola.

217. KURIMU KŌHĪ Hot Coffee with whipped cream on the top. Also called VIENNA COFFEE.

218. KURĪMU SŌDA Usually a green soda float. Vanilla icecream on top of a soda drink.

219. **MERON JŪSU** A green melon flavored drink made
with a sweet syrup and water.

220. **MIRUKU** Milk. (Tea room style, iced)

221. **MIRUKU SĒKI** A supposed "milk shake," but made
with milk, sugar and an egg.

222. **ORENJI FANTA** "Fanta" brand orange drink.

223. **ORENJI FURŌTO** Orange float. A soda drink with
orange flavoring and vanilla ice cream on top.

224. **ORENJI JŪSU** Orange flavored drink (carbonated.)
Occasionally, you can find fresh, real orange juice.

225. **PA-IN JŪSU** A pineapple drink (carbonated.)

226. **REMONĒDO** Lemonade, sweet and usually cold.

227. **REMON SUKASSHU** Lemon squash. A sweet soda
drink often with a cherry and lemon slice on top.

228. **SŌDA SUI** A green, sweet soda drink.

229. **TOMATO JŪSU** Canned tomato juice.

Milk Stand Drinks and Snacks

DRINKS

230. GYŪNYŪ "SHIRO" (White) Milk. Sometimes heated in the winter.

231. ICHIGO GYŪNYŪ Sweetened milk with strawberry essence (pink.)

232. KŌHĪ GYŪNYŪ Sweetened milk with artificial coffee flavoring (brown.) Sometimes heated in the winter.

233. ORENJI JŪSU Sweet orange juice made from real oranges but diluted.

234. RINGO JŪSU Sweetened apple juice made from real apples but diluted.

235. SOFUTO KŌHĪ Milk flavored with real coffee (in a tall soft drink bottle.)

236. SOFUTO SĒKI A sweet, light yellow milk drink made with egg and vanilla flavoring.

237. SOFUTO YŌGURUTO A sweetened yogurt drink.

238. TOMATO JŪSU Tomato juice.

YOGURT DESSERTS (*eaten with a spoon*)

239. ICHIGO YŌGURUTO Pink, sweetened yogurt flavored with strawberry essence.

240. ORENJI YŌGURUTO Orange flavored sweetened yogurt.

240. PA-IN YŌGURUTO Pineapple flavored sweetened yogurt.

241. YŌGURUTO White sweetened yogurt.

"EKI-BEN"

BOX LUNCHES . . . . . ON THE TRAIN

In addition to the speed of the long distance trains and the natural beauty of the countryside, one of the delights of train travel in Japan is the opportunity to eat a special kind of box lunch popularly called EKI-BEN. (O-BENTŌ is anyone's everyday box lunch, while the abbreviated EKI-BEN refers to the special train station lunch.) There are a variety of meals available in this lunch box form, including a few semi-Western combinations.

Most of the lunches are contained in thin, wooden boxes of various shapes and are wrapped with decorative paper and tied with a string. (According to accepted Japanese picnic behavior, all of this packaging must be kept carefully intact so the entire box can be re-wrapped in exactly the same way after eating.) In some places the container is an interestingly shaped pottery dish which can be kept as a souvenir and used for food or as a vase after your trip.

Lunch boxes are usually sold on train platforms, (near the boarding areas of the long distance trains at Shinjuku, Tokyo and Ueno Stations in Tokyo), and in shops around the stations of other cities and towns. In addition, EKI-BEN sellers will frequently call out their wares as they pass your window during brief station stops. Sometimes EKI-BEN lunches are sold in the aisle of the train along with the usual cold drinks (including not only juice and cola, but also SAKE, beer and whiskey). You may eat and drink at any hour of the day, as you may be surprised to discover the first time you see kimono-clad older ladies board the train and eagerly open their EKI-BEN lunches and cans of beer at 10:00 AM.

The first EKI-BEN, 2 rice balls and pickles wrapped in bamboo leaves, is said to have been sold at Utsunomiya Station 85 years ago; and today many stations and towns all over Japan are known for a particular kind of food sold in their EKI-BEN lunch. Knowledgeable travelers will wait for a particular stop in order to purchase a famous EKI-BEN. For example, Yokohama Station is known for the Chinese meat balls in SHŪ-MAI BENTŌ, and at Chiba Station you can buy YAKIHAMA BENTŌ, clams served over rice.

With some varieties of these lunches, hot green tea can be purchased. Traditionally the tea has been sold in charming pots made by local potters; and in a few places you may still collect one of these attractive souvenirs. However, in most large cities, regretably, the un-lovely plastic container with a green tea-bag has replaced the pottery.

The foods served in all of these lunches are prepared and distributed daily, and usually by early afternoon they are completely sold out. Once you become accustomed to the novelty of eating rice and bits of cooked fish and vegetables which are cold you are on your way to becoming a lunch box connoisseur. You may even want to visit Mitsukoshi or Keio Department Stores when they feature EKI-BEN Fairs once or twice a year. At Mitsukoshi, Ikebukuro branch, the Fair is held for about a week usually in February and November. About 30 of the most famous EKI-BEN lunches from all over Japan are made daily and sold to nostalgic Tokyo customers.

If you prefer travel by car instead of by train, you will find many of these same kinds of lunches available in shops at rest stop areas along the major cross-country highways. These are called by the general name, O-BENTO. One of the most famous of these is UNAGI BENTŌ (broiled eel) sold at Hamamatsu on the Tomei Kosoku Doro.

1. **EKI-BEN Lunches Sold in Train Stations in Tokyo**

    a. **CHIKIN BENTŌ** (Chicken Lunch)
       Tokyo Station

    b. **MAKUNO UCHI**
       Tokyo Station
       Ueno Station
       Shinjuku Station

    c. **OKONOMI ZUSHI**
       Tokyo Station

    d. **OSHIZUSHI**
       Ueno Station

    e. **O-SUSHI**
       Tokyo Station

    f. **SAIGO BENTO**
       Ueno Station

    g. **SANDO-ICHI**
       (Sandwich)
       Most stations
       in big cities

a

b

c

d

e

f

g

79

2. Some of the More Famous EKI-BEN Lunches

a. **HANAGASA ZUSHI** ......Yamagata Station, Yamagata
Prefecture

b. **MASU NO SUSHI** ....Toyama Station, Toyama
Prefecture

c. **NUKU ZUSHI** ....Okayama Station, Okayama
Prefecture

d. **TŌGE NO KAMAMESHI**..Yokokawa Station, Gunma
Prefecture

a

b

c

d

SAKE (polite O-SAKE)

TRADITIONAL JAPANESE WINES AND LIQUORS

SAKE The general Japanese name for any drink, traditional or imported, but usually used to refer to a white wine made from fermented rice. (Note: SAKE is well known to visitors to Japan but is often mispronounced to rhyme with "hockey;" to avoid misunderstanding it should be pronounced "Sa-Kay.")

SHŌ-CHŪ A distilled liquor (up to 90 proof) made from either sweet potatoes or rice, SHŌ-CHŪ is little known and rarely tasted by foreigners and is much malligned by Japanese who tend to regard SHŌ-CHŪ as a cheap, inferior drink. Actually, some of the best SHŌ-CHŪ (such as Kumajōchū) is an excellent pure liquor which compares favorably with the native liquors of other countries such as tequila, vodka, pisco, etc.

MIRIN A sweet wine made from SHŌ-CHŪ, high gluten rice and malted rice, essential in preparing many Japanese foods.

TOSO Served on New Year's Day in an elegant lacquered pot with a set of three graduated cups, this is a wine made by mixing SAKE with MIRIN and adding a silk bag containing a mixture of herbs. (The bag of herbs, sold in an elaborately wrapped paper envelope, is said to have special powers.) The drink is meant to drive away evil family spirits in order to begin the New Year propitiously.

UME-SHU Plum wine (or Apricot spirit, depending on how one defines UME) made during the summer in many households by putting green Japanese plums into SHŌ-CHŪ and adding sugar. UME-SHU must be aged for at least a year.

81

SAKE proudly claims an ancient history in Japan with strong religious and social meanings which are still retained today. From the custom of offering SAKE as a libation to the gods, the drinking parties of today evolved, though originally SAKE was prepared as a thick gruel to be eaten rather than drunk. Traditionally, every community shrine had its own rice fields, and it was from the rice harvested from these fields that SAKE was prepared and shared among the members of the farm community. One of the distinctive features of SAKE drinking is that SAKE is warmed to about body temperature (though some persons prefer cold SAKE in the summer); this custom of warming SAKE dates to about the Eighth Century.

The drinking of SAKE has always been considered an essential part of every Japanese festival and ceremonial occasion and it is still offered to the gods and ancestors in community and household shrines. It is also the essential part of the nuptial pledge in traditional wedding ceremonies, in which the bride and groom drink three times from each of three ceremonial cups (SANSAN KUDO). Even in very informal social gatherings and parties at restaurants, the sense of community and sharing of SAKE is retained. This feeling is expressed in a few "rules" about SAKE drinking which should be observed: one should never pour his own cup of SAKE—rather, another person fills your empty cup and you fill the cup of the other person, etc. Similarly, the cup being filled should be held and not just left setting on the table. (These same rules are usually extended to the drinking of beer and other social drinks.)

The making of SAKE requires pure water and a cold climate, and thus some people feel that although SAKE is made throughout Japan, the best SAKE comes from certain areas, such as Nada, Fushimi and Akita. Unlike Western wines, SAKE does not necessarily improve with age, and there are no "vintage years" for SAKE as there are for European wines. Today, the Japanese government requires that SAKE manufacturers present their products each spring to be examined and officially graded. Based on the taste, color and scent, SAKE is ranked:

Grade 1: TOKKYŪ-SHU ..the best quality (16–16.9 percent alcohol)
Grade 2: IKKYŪ-SHU ....the middle grade (15.5–16.5 percent alcohol)
Grade 3: NIKKYŪ-SHU ..the cheapest grade (15–15.9 percent alcohol).

SAKE is sold in a variety of containers and different sizes of

bottles, ranging from the very small, individual bottles dispensed in vending machines and sold at train stations, to the enormous straw-wrapped kegs often seen at shrines and sold as New Year's gifts. There are several standard size bottles but the most popular size is very large by Western standards, 1.8 liters (nearly a half-gallon). But if this bottle seems large, the pitchers in which SAKE is served seem unusually small and delicate. (Visitors to Japan often mistake SAKE pitchers for bud vases!) The variety of SAKE pitchers and cups is truly extraordinary and a set of these makes one of the most popular choices of gifts among the works of Japanese potters. SAKE is also sometimes drunk from small wooden boxes which were originally used as units of measure.

FOODS WITH SAKE

The simple elegance of SAKE servings is often enhanced by a variety of special tidbits to be taken with SAKE, foods known as SAKE NO SAKANA (polite), or OTSUMAMI. (Some of these foods are listed in this guide under A La Carte.) A stroll through the food section of any department store provides a tantalizing survey of some of these delights artfully displayed. Columns of tiny dried and seasoned seafoods on skewers; sweet-salty dried cuttlefish; and many more such "snacks" are as pleasing to the eye as to the taste. In a restaurant some of these, as well as SASHIMI, are often served with SAKE.

83

1   2   3

ABOUT JAPANESE TEA
"O-CHA"

Green tea, the symbol of gracious hospitality and ancient tradition, is perhaps the most familiar of all Japanese restaurant offerings. A cup arrives at your table before you order, and again at the end of your meal, never with a charge. A few shops and most stores which sell tea offer a friendly cup to their customers.

Visitors often do not realize how significant tea is in Japan. If one travels away from the city, he will see beautiful rolling hillsides of dark green tea bushes which at first look like vast sculptured gardens. Tea bushes are common in the gardens of many homes, even in Tokyo, and most farm families grow a hedge or two of tea for their daily use. The Tea Ceremony, a ritual with deep cultural significance in Japan, continues to be studied by many men and women in Japan today. This aesthetic and spiritual tradition is derived from ancient Buddhist customs. Tea in the Tea Ceremony, by the way, is a powdered, green tea whisked into a froth and served in large, ceremonial tea bowls. Even the medical value of green tea has been known for centuries: O-CHA contains more vitamin C than the tea usually served in Western countries. In some ways, tea in Japan epitomizes the spirit of Japanese cooking: simple, nutritious, aesthetically pleasing and symbolic of deep cultural heritage.

The freshly picked leaves of Japanese tea are kept green by a process of steaming and heating to prevent oxidation. Unlike black tea, green tea is not fermented. Tea leaves are classified according to the way they are grown and picked; the best and most expensive kind of tea is made from the tenderest young leaves cut from older bushes grown in the shade. Japanese tea is never served or drunk with sugar except for a summer iced drink made from powdered tea.

84

5　　　　　　　　　　　7

4　　　　　　　　6

There are six kinds of Japanese tea; however in traditional tea shops you will have a choice of two or three grades and prices of each type.

HIKICHA (also called **MATCHA**)　Powdered green tea (used int he Tea Ceremony) made from the young leaves of aged tea plants. The leaves are dried and then ground in a stone mortar. The tea is whipped in hot water with a delicate bamboo whisk in the same bowl in which it is served. (Picture No. 1)

GYOKURO　The best and most expensive grade of leaves are used in this tea. The flavor is mild and slightly sweet when it is brewed correctly in water of 60 to 70 degrees C. for one or two minutes. (Picture No. 2)

SENCHA　The most common tea, medium priced and usually served to guests. The leaves are tender but are grown larger than HIKICHA leaves. It should be brewed for only one minute in 75 or 80 degree C. water. This tea is ferquently served with SUSHI. (Picture No. 3)

BANCHA　The cheapest tea made from larger tougher leaves which are cut to include the stems. It should be brewed for at least one minute in water 85 to 100 degrees C. (Picture No. 4)

HOJICHA　These are the same leaves used for BANCHA, but they are roasted, giving them a brownish color and a distinct smoky flavor. (Picture No. 5)

GENMAICHA　BANCHA mixed with roasted and popped rice. (Picture No. 6)

MUGICHA　Not really a tea, but rather a drink made from roasted barley and usually served cool. It is a golden color and is a popular summer drink. (Picture No. 7)

KOBU CHA　Made from powdered seaweed. (It tastes like a salted soup.)

HABU CHA　Stinkweed-seed tea.

SAKURA YU　Made with salty pickled cherry blossoms and drunk on some ceremonial occasions.

85

Tori no Ichi Festival at Ōtori Shrine in Tokyo

STREET AND FESTIVAL FOODS

It used to be, not so very long ago, that the streets of Tokyo and Kyoto were filled with the cries and chants of street vendors offering their freshly cooked and deliciously smelling fishes, noodles, snacks and sweets. Today it is still possible to sample many of the same street-side snacks in a few neighborhoods or along the narrow, winding streets which surround the larger train stations and shopping centers. An even better way, however, is to locate the site of a temple or shrine festival (several of which are held each month in most large cities). The colorful celebrations during these occasions are held in the midst of a great variety of small stalls selling these very foods.

1. WANDERING WAGONS.... Hand or bicycle pulled.

ODEN An open wagon with a steaming container of hot fish and vegetable cakes, hard boiled eggs, seaweed, TOFU and sometimes octopus bubbling in a broth. Each piece is served on a bamboo skewer or as a standard plate combination called "HITO-SARA." A side dab of hot mustard is included. Prices are per stick or plate.

RĀMEN Two notes on an old fashioned Japanese flute will announce the arrival of this wagon-stand. Step right up ... serves two or three or a crowd of five, a steaming bowl of yellow noodles in a broth. No choice, just RĀMEN.

YAKI-IMO "Baked Yam" Wagon
A wonderful, hand pulled, boxy cart complete with chimney, which carries a bed of pebbles heated by a wood fire underneath. Your hot, baked yam will be dug out from under the stones and weighed on a tiny scale. Prices vary . . . (Buy a big one). The call can be heard 3 streets away, a long, sung out YAaaa, KIiii, IMOoo.

2. STREET STANDS....More or Less Stationary

RĀMEN More elaborate than the wagon variety. You will be invited to duck under the "doorway" curtain hanging over the front of the stand, and order from a choice of 2 or 3 noodle dishes; usually RĀMEN (see listing No. 52), TANMEN (No. 56), MOYASHI SOBA (No. 46) or MISO RĀMEN (No. 44).

SOBA Hot and cold Japanese buckwheat noodle dishes can be purchased from these stands. The usual choice is KAKE SOBA (No. 36) and TSUKIMI SOBA (No. 61). (See lower left photo.)

TAKO YAKI Purchased by the containerful (9 to 12 in a box). These are griddle fried dumplings made from a wheat batter containing bits of cooked octopus, green onion and ginger. Spoonfuls are baked into a ball while you watch. A spicy sauce and a sprinkle of dried seaweed are added on top. The dumplings are to be eaten with a toothpick conveniently supplied in the side of the box. TAKO YAKI may be eaten at the stand or carried home. (See lower right photo.)

AMAGURI Roasted Chinese chestnuts. (See photo above.)

BEKKO AME Candy suckers moulded on a griddle as you watch.

DARUMA SEMBEI A very large cracker in the shape of a DARUMA made from rice.

IKA YAKI Charcoal grilled squid with a coating of soy sauce eaten whole on a wooden skewer. (See lower left photo.)

KARAMERU YAKI Large, round, cookie-like puffs of brown sugar made in a ladle heated over a fire.

SAIKU AME White, green and pink colored candy. Sometimes shaped like balls or long sticks or DARUMA dolls.

MIKAN BEKKŌ Candy coated fruits (whole tangerine or apple, or small pieces of any fruit.) (See lower right photo.)

MITARASHI DANGO 4 skewered rice flour dumplings, broiled over charcoal and dipped in a soy sauce.

OKONOMI YAKI Seasoned, hot pancake; stands sell cheaper versions of the kind offered in specialty restaurants. (See listing No. 151.)

OKOSHI
Traditional popped rice candy.

YAKI TORI
Barbecued chicken snack.

OKOSHI Pink, green, or brown sugar coated popped rice in various shapes; DARUMA dolls, rectangles, kettles, etc.

TAI YAKI Rather large, fish shaped pancakes, stuffed with a generous amount of sweet, soy bean jam.

TAKO SEMBEI A large pink cracker with a dried shrimp, octopus or cuttlefish flavor.

TŌMOROKOSHI Roasted corn on the cob. Sometimes seasoned with soy sauce.

YAKI TORI Small pieces of cheap chicken (or chicken liver . . . "REBA") on a bamboo skewer, broiled over charcoal and dipped in a special sauce.

YAKI SOBA (see listing No. 64)

YASAI SEMBEI Very sweet and colorful small candies shaped as various vegetables.

WATAGASHI Cotton candy (spun sugar).

APPENDIX (I)

Japanese Phrases
for Restaurant Use

(See pronunciation guide on page 6. Don't forget to read "I" as ee.)

What's the name of this? (dish, food)

KORE WA NAN DES KA?

Do you have this? (point to picture)

KORE WA ARIMAS KA?

Should I buy a ticket before eating?

SHOKKEN O KAU NO DES KA?

What is good today?

KYŌ WA NANI GA OISHII DES KA?

Does it take long to prepare?

JIKAN GA KAKARIMAS KA?

How much is this? (price)

KORE WA IKURA DES KA?

How much is the bill?

IKURA DES KA?

I don't understand.

WAKARI-MASEN.

Please show me the check.

DENPYŌ MISETE KUDASAI.

Do you speak English?

EGO GA DEKIMAS KA?

What's the name of this restaurant?

KONO MISE NO NAMAE WA NAN DES KA?

What time do you open?

MISE WA NANJI NI AKIMAS KA?

What time do you close?

MISE WA NANJI NI SHIMEMAS KA?

Please give me a glass of water.

OMIZU KUDASAI.

Please give me a knife and fork.

NAIFU TO FŌKU KUDASAI.

Please give me another (one of anything)

MO-HITOTSU KUDASAI.

(In Tokyo HITOTSU sounds like "SHTOTSU")

Where is the restroom?

TOIRE WA DOKO DES KA?

(Most small restaurants have only a single restroom.)

Where is a public telephone?

    KŌSHŪ DENWA WA DOKO DES KA?

Where is the nearest train station?

    ICHIBAN CHIKAI EKI WA DOKO DES KA?

Please draw a map for me.

    CHIZU O KAITE KUDASAI.

Please call a taxi for me.

    TAKUSHĪ O YONDE KUDASAI.

How to Read Japanese Prices:

十　円.............	10 yen	(JŪ EN)
五十円.............	50 yen	(GOJŪ EN)
百　円.............	100 yen	(HYAKU EN)
二百円.............	200 yen	(NI-HYAKU EN)
三百円.............	300 yen	(SAN-BYAKU EN)
四百円.............	400 yen	(YON-HYAKU EN)
五百円.............	500 yen	(GO-HYAKU EN)
千　円.............	1,000 yen	(SEN YEN)
五千円.............	5,000 yen	(GO-SEN YEN)
一万円.............	10,000 yen	(ICHI-MAN YEN)

Useful Vocabulary:

Yes	HAI
No	IIE
Please say it again	MŌ ICHI-DO ITTE KUDASAI.
Chopsticks	HASHI (polite O-HASHI)
OSHIBORI	A rolled, damp washcloth for wiping hands and face. (The individual cloth is offered hot in the winter and cold in the summer.)
ITADAKIMAS	"Bon appetit"....Said before eating.
GOCHISŌ-SAMA-DESHITA	Said at the end of a meal. It means roughly, "thank you, I have eaten well".
OKAWARI	A second helping (drink, food, etc.)
SUKOSHI	A little bit.

91

APPENDIX (II)

A Glossary of Japanese Foods

ABURAGE ....Thin, deep fried soybean curd.

AKAENDO ....Beans used whole in various kinds of traditional Japanese desserts.

AN ....Bean jam made from redbeans

AZUKI ....Red beans (small).

CHIKUWA ....Bamboo shaped, broiled fish cake.

CHIRIZU ....A spicy, soup-like dip made from soy sauce, DASHI and citron juice.

DAIKON ....Giant, white radish often served in a tiny grated mound to be used as a seasoning.

DAIZU ....Soybeans.

DASHI ....The basic Japanese soup stock made from dried bonito shavings or tangle seaweed.

DENBU ....Pink, or brown, sweet, cooked ground fish.

FU ....Dried bread-like pieces of wheat gluten.

GOMA ....Sesame seeds.

HANPEN ....Soft, white, boiled fish cake.

HARUSAME ....Vermicelli. (The Japanese name means "spring rain".)

KAMABOKO ....Steamed fish cake often with a pink edge, usually eaten in slices.

KAMPYŌ ....Dried gourd shavings.

KANTEN ....Gelatin made from seaweed called TENGUSA.

KATAKURIKO ......Potato starch.

KATSUOBUSHI ......Dried bonito fish. (Looks like a piece of driftwood.)

KIKURAGE ....Edible tree fungus.

KINAKO ....Yellow, powdered soybeans, often used on Japanese desserts. (Not sweet.)

KONBU ....Tangle; wide leafed seaweed.

KONNYAKU ....Gelatin cubes or strips made from arum root.

KONOME ....Japanese pepper leaves used for decoration and flavor. They symbolize spring.

KUZUKO ....Powdered arrowroot.

MIRIN	Japanese sweet rice wine for cooking.
MISO	Yellow, or brown fermented soybean paste. It is the main seasoning for many soup, vegetable and fish dishes.
MISOSHIRU	The soup made from MISO. (see listing No. 120)
MITSUBA	Trefoil; delicate leaves used for decoration and flavor.
MOCHI	Japanese rice cake, traditionally eaten to celebrate the New Year.
MYŌGA	Buds of the MYŌGA plant (Zingiber Mioga) eaten in soup or as a vegetable.
NARUTO	Round, boiled fish cake with a pink swirl inside, eaten in slices.
NORI	Dried lavor (seaweed) crispy and delicious.
PONZU	Citron juice.
SAKE	Japanese rice wine.
SANSHO	A kind of Japanese pepper (not hot, rather herb-like).
SASHIMI	Sliced, very fresh, raw fish.
SATSUMA AGE	Deep fried fish cake.
SEMBEI	Many kinds of Japanese rice crackers.
SHIITAKE	Large, flat mushroom, fresh or dried.
SHINACHIKU	Salted Chinese bamboo.
SHŌYU	Soy sauce. (originally brought from China in the 6th century by Buddhist priests.) It is made from soybeans, barley and salt.
SHUNGIKU	Edible chrysanthemum leaves.
SOBA	See Page 23.
TAKUWAN	Yellow pickles (slices) made from radish.
TEMPURA	Deep fried fish & vegetables. See page 20.
TOFU	Soft, white, bean curd cake.
UDON	See page 24.
UZURA TAMAGO	Quail egg.
WASABI	Horseradish, green, used freshly grated as a seasoning for SASHIMI, SUSHI, etc. (See page 41.)
WAKAME	Seaweed, smaller than tangle, eaten in soups and vegetable dishes.
YUZU	Citron. A small slice of the peel is often used for flavoring in soup.

APPENDIX (III)

English Names of Common Foods, and How to Pronounce Them Like a Japanese

(See pronunciation guide in the introduction, page 6.   Don't forget to read "I" as ee.)

(Beef) Steak	BIFU TEKI
Beer	BĪ-RU
Butter	BA-TĀ
Bread	PAN
Cake	KEI-KI
Coffee	KŌ-HĪ
Cola	KŌ-RA
Cheese	CHĪ-ZU
Curried Rice	KARĒ RA-I-SU
Fried Shrimp	EBI FU-RA-I
Fried Oyster	KAKI FU-RA-I
Hamburger	HAM-BĀ-GU
Ham	HA-MU
Hot Dog	HOTTO DOGGU
Icecream	A-I-SU KURĪMU
Icecream Cone (soft, icemilk)	SO-FU-TO KURĪMU
Lemon	REMON
Liver	REBĀ
Milk	MI-RU-KU
Pork Cutlet	TON-KATSU
Rice	RA-I-SU (also GO-HAN)
Salad	SA-RA-DA
Sandwich	SAN-DO-ICHI
Soup	POTĀJU (any thick, Western soup)
	KONSOME (any thin, Western soup)
Water	O-HIYA (a glass of cold water)
	O-MIZU (water, a general term)
	OYU (hot water)

APPENDIX (IV)

Fish List

AJI	Pompano, Horse Mackerel
AMADAI	Tilefish
ANAGO	Conger Eel
ANKO	Angler
ASARI	Short Necked Clam
AWABI	Abalone
AYU	Japanese River Trout
BORA	Gray Mullet
BURI	Yellow Tail
DOJŌ	Loach
EBI	Shrimp
ISE EBI	Lobster, Crayfish
KURUMA EBI	Prawn
SHIBA EBI	Tiny Shrimp
FUGU	Blowfish
FUKA	A kind of Shark
FUNA	Crucian Carp
HAMACHI	Young Yellow Tail
HAMAGURI	Clam
HAZE	Mudfish
HIRAME	Flatfish, Flounder
HOTATE GAI	Scallops
HŌBŌ	Gurnard, Gurnet
IIDAKO	Baby Octopus
IKA	Squid, Cuttlefish
INADA	Round Yellow Tail
IWASHI	Sardine
KAJIKI MAGURO	Swordfish
KAKI	Oyster
KAMASU	Pike
KANI	Crab
KARASUMI	Dried Roe
KAREI	Flatfish
KATSUO	Bonito
KISU	Sillago
KOCHI	Flathead
KOHADA	A kind of large Sardine
KOI	Carp
KUJIRA	Whale

MAGURO (no akami)	Tuna (red)
MANA GATSUO	Butter Fish
MASU	Lake Trout
NIJIMASU	Rainbow Trout
NISHIN	Herring
SABA	Mackerel
SAKE (SHAKE)	Salmon
SAME	Shark
SAMMA	Pike, Saury
SAWARA	Mackerel
SAYORI	Halfbeak
SAZAE	Wreath Shell, Top Shell
SHAKO	Mantis Shrimp
SHIRASU	Very tiny white fish
SHIRAUO	Very small, translucent fish
SUZUKI	Sea Bass
SUZUKO	Fish Roe
TAI	Sea Bream, Red Snapper
TAKO	Octopus
TARA	Cod Fish
TARAKO	Cod Roe
TOBIUO	Flying Fish
TORO	Light, pinkish Tuna.
UNAGI	Eel
UNI	The eggs of Sea Chestnuts or Sea Urchins.

MASU (Lake Trout)

KURUMA EBI
(Prawn)

MAGURO (Tuna)

EBI (Shrimp)

SHAKE (Salmon)

APPENDIX (V)

Index

(Numbers in italic refer to pages and those in roman to food listing numbers.)

99

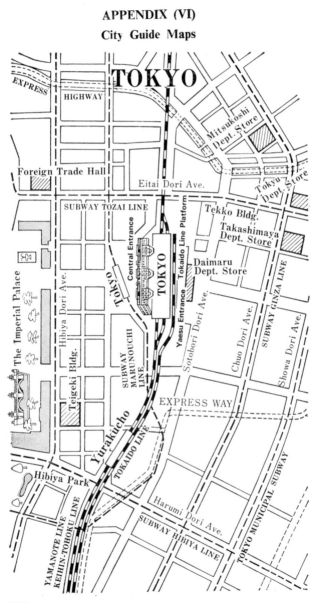

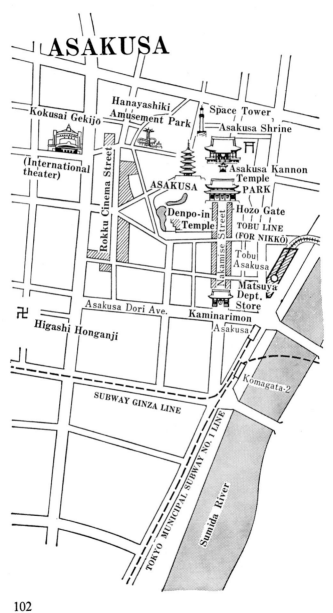

ASAKUSA

Kokusai Gekijo
(International theater)

Hanayashiki Amusement Park

Space Tower

Asakusa Shrine

Asakusa Kannon Temple

ASAKUSA PARK

Rokku Cinema Street

Denpo-in Temple

Hozo Gate

TOBU LINE (FOR NIKKÔ)

Nakamise Street

Tobu Asakusa

Matsuya Dept. Store

Asakusa Dori Ave.

Kaminarimon

Higashi Honganji

Asakusa

Komagata-2

SUBWAY GINZA LINE

TOKYO MUNICIPAL SUBWAY NO. 1 LINE

Sumida River

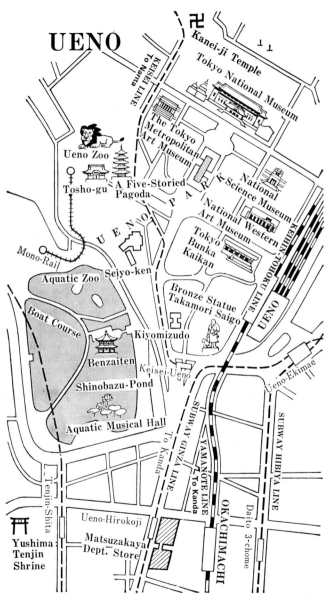

UENO

To Nature — KEISEI LINE

卍 Kanei-ji Temple

⊥⊥

Tokyo National Museum

The Tokyo Metropolitan Art Museum

Ueno Zoo

Tosho-gu

A Five-Storied Pagoda

National Science Museum

U E N O   P A R K

National Western Art Museum

Tokyo Bunka Kaikan

KEIHIN-TOHOKU LINE

Mono-Rail

Aquatic Zoo   Seiyo-ken

Boat Course

Benzaiten

Kiyomizudo

Shinobazu-Pond

Aquatic Musical Hall

Bronze Statue Takamori Saigo

UENO

Keisei-Ueno

Ueno-Ekimae

SUBWAY HIBIYA LINE

To Kanda

SUBWAY GINZA LINE

YAMANOTE LINE
To Kanda

OKACHIMACHI

Daito 3-chome

Tenjin-Shita

鳥居 Yushima Tenjin Shrine

Ueno-Hirokoji

Matsuzakaya Dept. Store

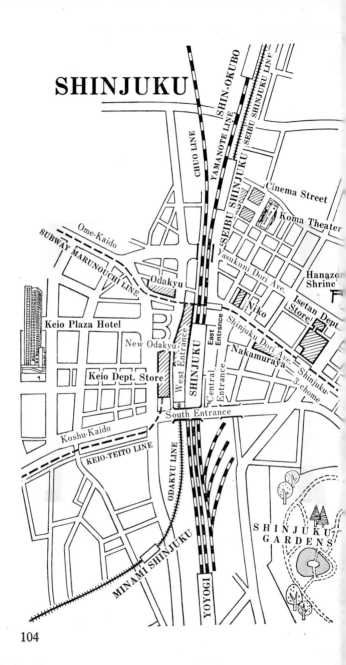

SHINJUKU

CHUO LINE

SHIN-OKUBO

YAMANOTE LINE

SEIBU SHINJUKU LINE

SEIBU SHINJUKU

Cinema Street

Koma Theater

Ome-Kaido

SUBWAY MARUNOUCHI LINE

Yasukuni Dori Ave.

Hanazono Shrine

Odakyu

Niko

Isetan Dept. Store

Keio Plaza Hotel

New Odakyu

Shinjuku Dori Ave.

Shinjuku-3 chome

Nakamuraya

West Entrance

East Entrance

SHINJUKU

Central Entrance

Keio Dept. Store

South Entrance

Koshu-Kaido

ODAKYU LINE

KEIO-TEITO LINE

SHINJUKU GARDENS

MINAMI SHINJUKU

YOYOGI

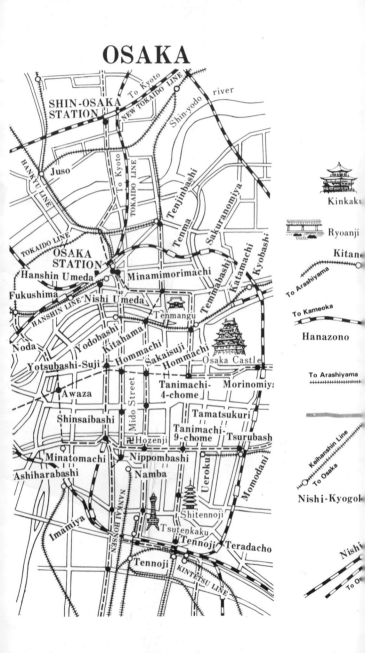